A-Z

BANGOR, ~~CON~~
COLWYN BA~~Y~~

CONTENTS

Key to Map Pages *allwedd i dudalennau'r map*	2-3
Map Pages *tudalennau'r map*	4-38
	9-48

REFERENCE *cyfeirnod*

A Road *ffordd A*	A55
Under Construction *wrthi'n cael ei adeiladu*	
Tunnel *twnel*	
B Road *ffordd B*	B5115
Dual Carriageway *ffordd ddeuol*	
One Way Street Traffic flow on A Roads is indicated by a heavy line on the driver's left. *stryd un ffordd* *nodir llif traffig ar ffyrdd A gan linell drom ar ochr chwith y gyrrwr*	➡
Restricted Access *Mynediad cyfyngedig*	
Pedestrianized Road *ffordd wedi ei phedestraneiddio*	
Track / Footpath *trac / llwybr*	
Residential Walkway *llwybr preswylwyr*	
Railway *rheilffordd*	Station *gorsaf* Heritage Sta. *gorsaf treftadaeth* Tunnel *twnel* Level Crossing *croesfa wastad*
Tramway *Llinell tramiau*	The boarding of trams at stations may be limited to a single direction, indicated by an arrow. *Mae'n bosib mai dim ond i un cyfeiriad y mae tram yn teithio o orsaf, ac fe nodir hynny gyda saeth.*
Built Up Area *ardal adeiledig*	BRICK ST.
Local Authority Boundary *ffin awdurdod lleol*	— ∙ — ∙ —
Postcode Boundary *ffin cod post*	— — —
Snowdonia National Park Boundary *ffin Parc Cenedlaethol Eryri*	
Map Continuation *parhad map*	15

Car Park selected *maes parcio* dethol	🅿
Church or Chapel *eglwys neu gapel*	†
Cycle Route selected *llwybr beic* dethol	🚲
Fire Station *gorsaf dân*	■
Hospital *ysbyty*	🅗
House Numbers A & B Roads only *rhifau tai* ffyrdd A & B	13 8
Information Centre *canolfan wybodaeth*	🅸
National Grid Reference *cyfeirnod grid cenedlaethol*	²85
Police Station *gorsaf heddlu*	▲
Post Office *swyddfa bost*	★
Toilet *toiled*	▽
with facilities for the Disabled *gyda chyfleusterau i'r anabl*	♿
Viewpoint *golygfan*	⁂ ※
Educational Establishment *sefydliad addysgol*	▢
Hospital *ysbyty*	▢
Industrial Building *adeilad diwydiannol*	▢
Leisure or Recreational Facility *cyfleusterau hamdden neu adloniant*	▢
Place of Interest *man diddorol*	▢
Public Building *adeilad cyhoeddus*	▢
Shopping Centre or Market *canolfan siopa neu farchnad*	▢
Other Selected Buildings *adeiladau dethol eraill*	▢

Scale 1:19,000 *graddfa*

0	¼	½ Mile *milltir*	3⅓ inches (8.47 cm) to 1 mile 5.26 cm to 1 kilometre
0 250 500 750 Metres *metr*		1 Kilometre *kilometr*	3⅓ modfeddi (8.47 cm) i 1 milltir 5.26 cm i 1 kilometr

Copyright of Geographers' A-Z Map Company Limited

Head Office *(prif swyddfa):*
Fairfield Road, Borough Green, Sevenoaks, Kent TN15 8PP
Telephone *(ffôn):* 01732 781000

Showrooms *(ystafelloedd arddangos):*
44 Gray's Inn Road, London WC1X 8HX
Telephone *(ffôn):* 020 7440 9500

Edition *(rhifyn)* 1 2000   Edition *(rhifyn)* 1b 2003
Copyright *(hawlfraint)* © Geographers' A-Z Map Co. Ltd. 2003

www.a-zmaps.co.uk

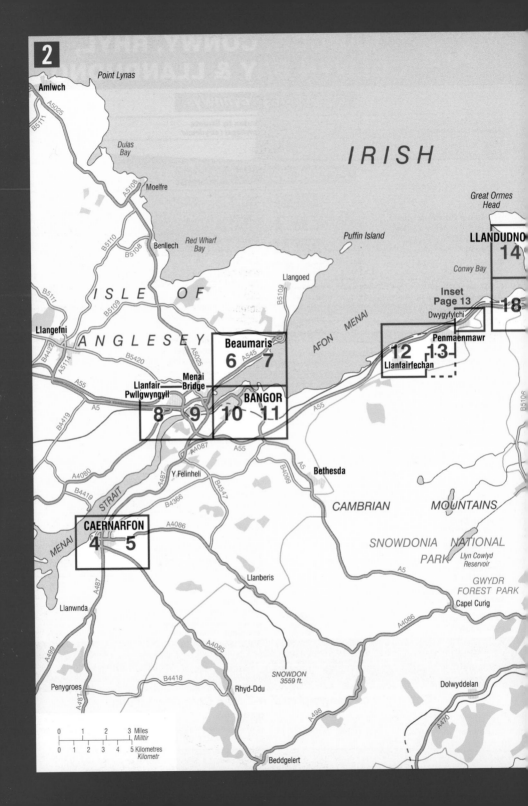

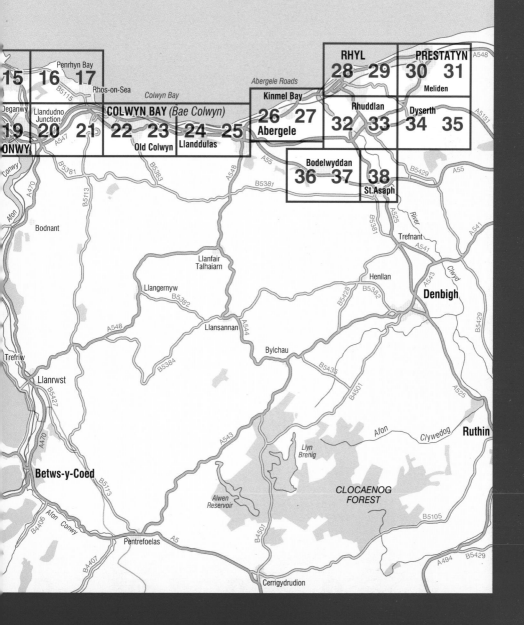

SEA

15	16	17

Penrhyn Bay
B5115
Rhos-on-Sea
Colwyn Bay
Abergele Roads

19	20	21	22	23	24	25

Deganwy
ONWY
Llandudno Junction
A547
COLWYN BAY *(Bae Colwyn)*
Old Colwyn
Llanddulas

Kinmel Bay

26	27
Abergele

RHYL

28	29

Rhuddlan

32	33

PRESTATYN

30	31

Meliden
Dyserth

34	35

Bodelwyddan

36	37	38
St.Asaph

A548
B5381
A55
B5381
B5383
A525
River
B5429
A55
A541
Clwyd
A5151
A548

Conwy
Afon
B5381
A470

Bodnant

Llanfair Talhaiarn

Llangernyw
B5392

Trefnant
A541
A543

Henllan
B5428
B5382

Denbigh

A543
B5429

Llansannan
A544

Trefriw

Llanrwst
B5384
A525

Bylchau
B5435
B4501

Ruthin

A470
B5427

Afon
Clywedog

Betws-y-Coed
B5173

Llyn Brenig

CLOCAENOG FOREST

Alwen Reservoir

A543
B4406
Afon Conwy

Pentrefoelas
A5
B4501
B5105

B4407
A494
B5429

Cerrigydrudion

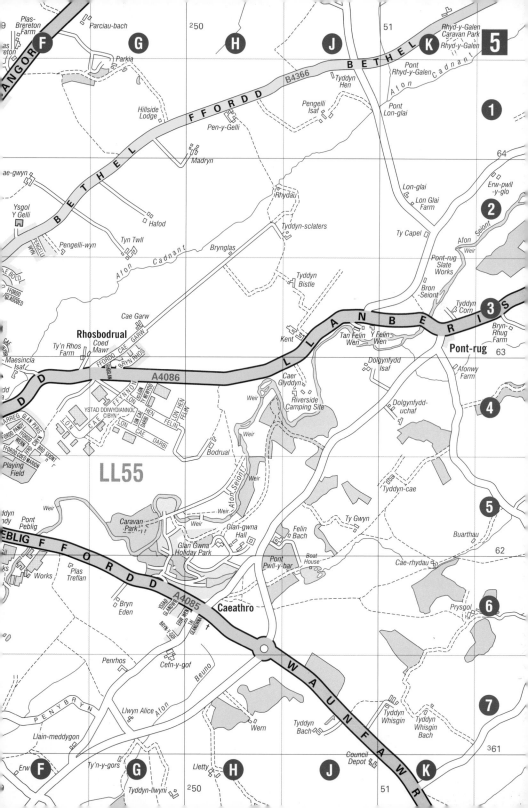

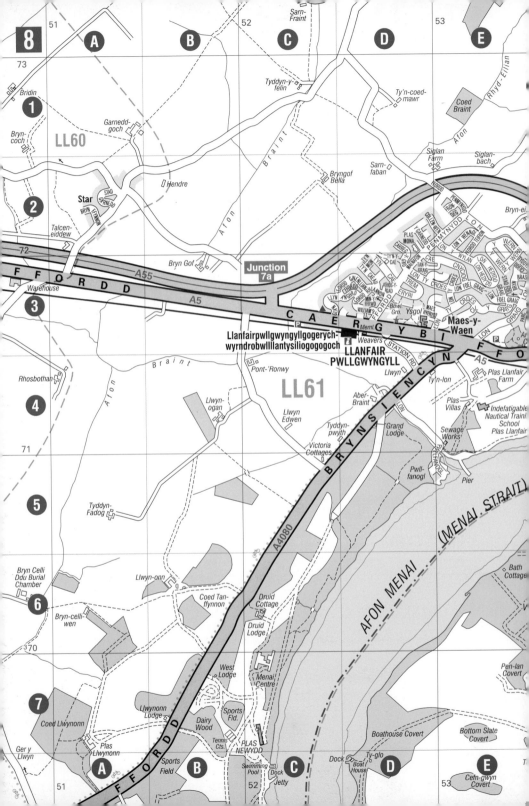

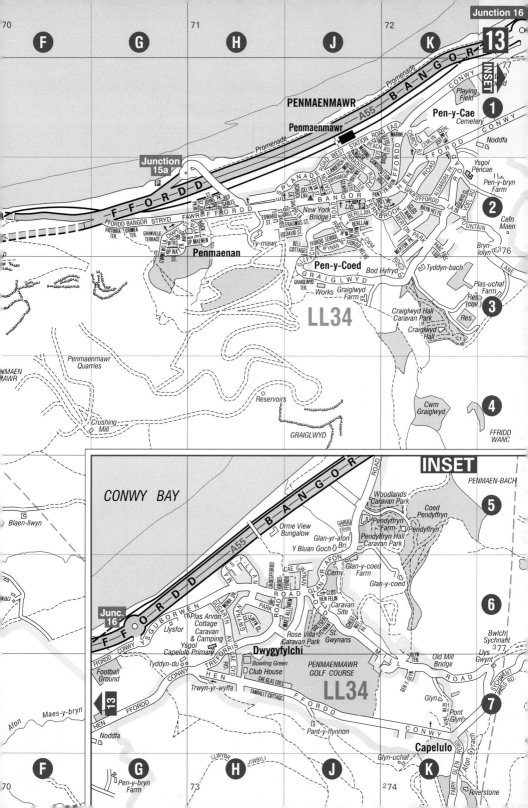

A B C D E

GREAT ORME

GREAT ORME
COUNTRY PARK &
NATURE RESERVE

Parc

Great Orme Country Park
Visitor Centre

Cemetery
Picnic
Site

ST. TUDNO'S

Porth yr
Helyg

Ffynnon Powel

Bryniau
Poethion

Llandudno Cable Car

Penmynydd Isa

Penmynydd
Uchan

TRWYNYGOGARTH

1

Great Orme Tramway

BISHOPS

Great
Orme
Mines

TY-GWYN

ROAD

ROAD MYTHOLROG

83

MONKS PATH

Ffynnon
Llygaid

Ffynnon
Gogarth

The Old
Abbey

Bishop's Quarries
(disused)

QUARRY

Pyllau

PYLLAU ROAD

Maes-y-facrell

Pen-y-gwaith

CROMLECH
RD.

ST. BUENO'S

Landing
Stage

Swn-y-Mor

2

Gogarth

Chapel
House

Pen-y-ffridd

Pant-y-ffridd

Pen-y-ffridd
Farm

CYLL
TERRACE

WYNNOR

TYN-Y-COED

Mini
Golf C

ANGLESEY RD

Playing Fld.

Hav
Gard

3

Ogof Arth

Loreto
St. Davids Convent
Hospice

INVALIDS

Toll Gate
Lodge

ABBEY

ABBEY PL

CYLL
CT

GLOF

Rec
Grd

GREAT ORMES RD

GWYDDFID AV.

MORFA

82

C O N W Y

4

DRIVE ABBEY WEST

PROMENADE WEST

GREAT ORMES RD

DALE RD.

LLOYD

PARADE

HOLYROOD
COURT

B A Y

5

CONWY SANDS

Sewage
Pumping Station

81

6

Tremlyd Point

NOR
GO

7

380

A B C D E

18

AFON CO

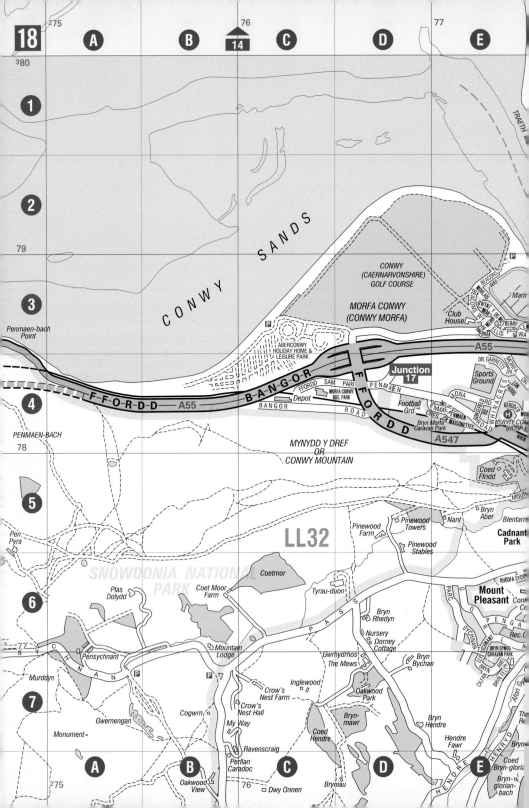

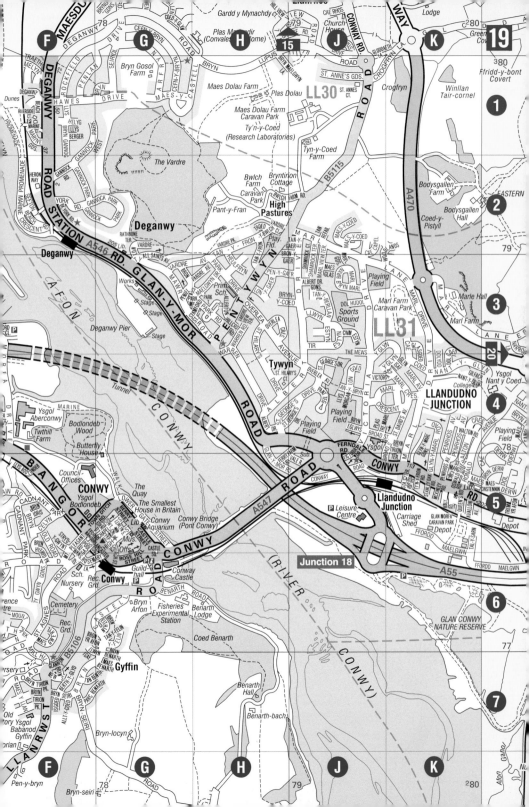

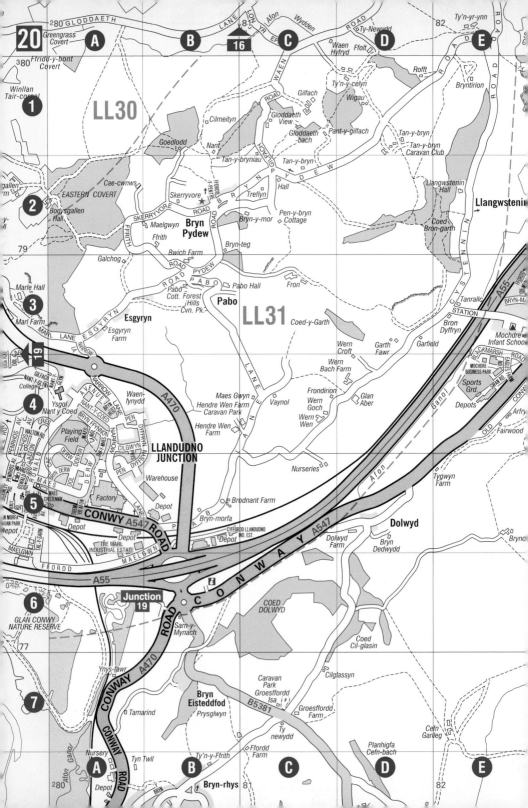

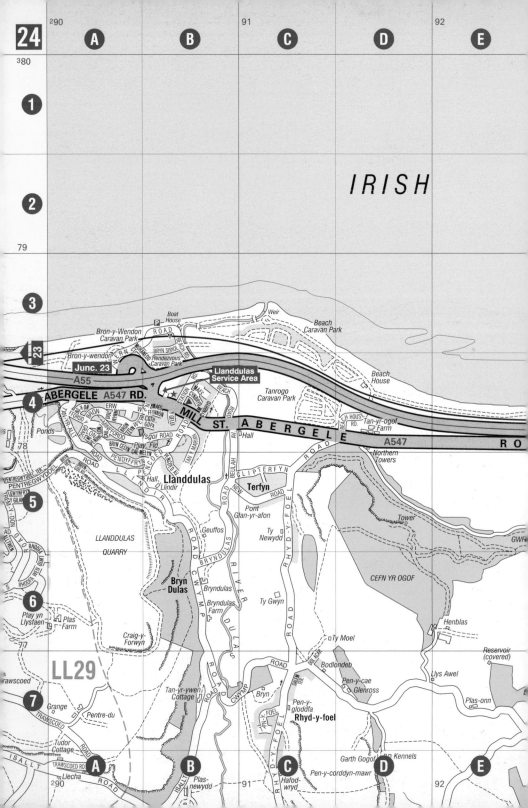

IRISH SEA

LL22

Kerfoots Caravan P
Abbeyford Country Club
Gaingc Holiday Pk.
Millers Caravan Park
Sandy Bay Cvn. Pk.
Morris's Holiday Camp
Edwards Leisure Park
Comm. Cen
Golden Gate Holiday Centre
Cambria Caravan Park
Browns Holiday Pk
Gainc-bach
Owen's Gainc Bach
Inter Leisure Holiday Park
Ty Gwyn Caravan Park
Caravan Park
Henllys
Ty-gwyn
Ty Mawr Holiday Park
Henllys Farm Camping & Touring Site
NORTH WALES HOLIDAY CAMP
PLASTIRION Pk.

ROAD TOWYN
PENISAF
SAN REMO
SANDBANK
BRYN
MAES Y LLAN
WENDORAN
MOR
PEN
PLASTIRION
MAES Y CASTELL
MAES RHASIN
TOWYN
WA
Pou Hou

A548

Kingsley Caravan Park
Harts Caravan Park
Sewage Works
FFORDD GWELFRYN
LON GLANFOR
LON-Y-DRYW
TREM-Y-MYNYDD
FFORDD HELYG
PARK
SEAFIELD
BRYN GELE
MAES GEIR
LON GLYD
LON Y WYLAN
MAES Y MOR
CREGYN
SUNRAY
MOLLAND DR.
NICHOLAS
Belgrano

TOWYN
GORS
ANNEDDLE
CAY NANT
MARINE
KINMEL
MORLAIS
LON Y ENCIL
CAER GLAN
Pensarn
Caravan Park
LON
MAES
CYB
FFORDD
PEN-MAES
MAES CANOL
Play Fld
Ysgolion
Maes Canol

MORFA RHUDDLAN

River Gele

A55

Sub

Junction 24

BRIDGE ST. RHUDDLAN RD.
RHUDDLAN RD.
A547
Cricket Ground
Playing Field
Ysgol
Pen-y-ffordd
Gofer

96
97

81
380
79

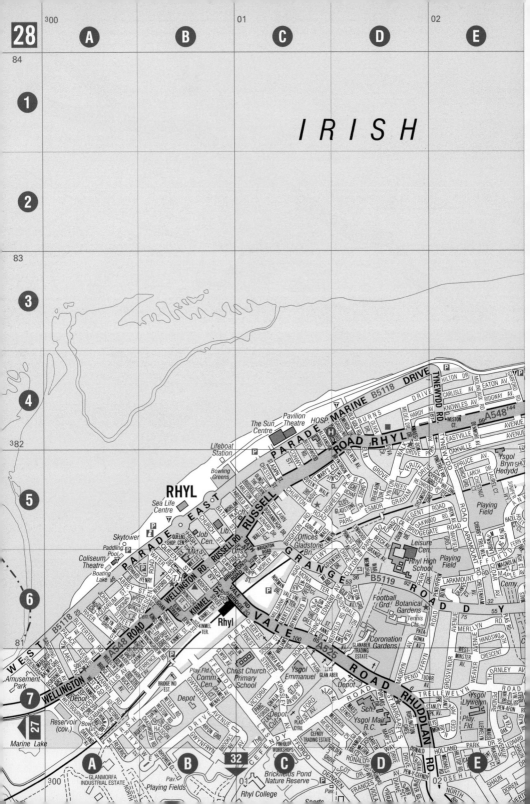

300   A   B   01   C   D   02   E

84

1

I R I S H

2

83

3

382

4

RHYL

83

Pavilion
Theatre

The Sun
Centre

HOSP.

PARADE MARINE B5118 DRIVE TYNEWYDD RD.

Lifeboat
Station

ROAD RHYL

Bowling
Greens

5

RHYL

Sea Life
Centre

Job
Cen.

Skytower

Paddling
Pool

Coliseum
Theatre

Boating
Lake

PARADE EAST

RUSSELL RD.

RUSSELL

GRANGE

Gladstone
Offices

Leisure
Cen.

Rhyl High
School

Playing
Field

Playing
Field

6

B5118 ROAD

A548 ROAD

WELLINGTON

KINMEL

Rhyl

VALE

B5119

Football
Grd.

Botanical
Gardens

Coronation
Gardens

Tennis
Cts.

81

WEST

Amusement
Park

WELLINGTON

Depot

Reservoir
(cov.)

Marine Lake

7

27

A525 ROAD RHUDDLAN RD.

Christ Church
Primary
School

Ysgol
Emmanuel

Ysgol Mair
R.C.

Ysgol
Llywelyn

A   B   32   C   D   E

Glanmorfa
Industrial Estate

300

Pav.
Playing Fields

01

Bricknells Pond
Nature Reserve

Rhyl College

02

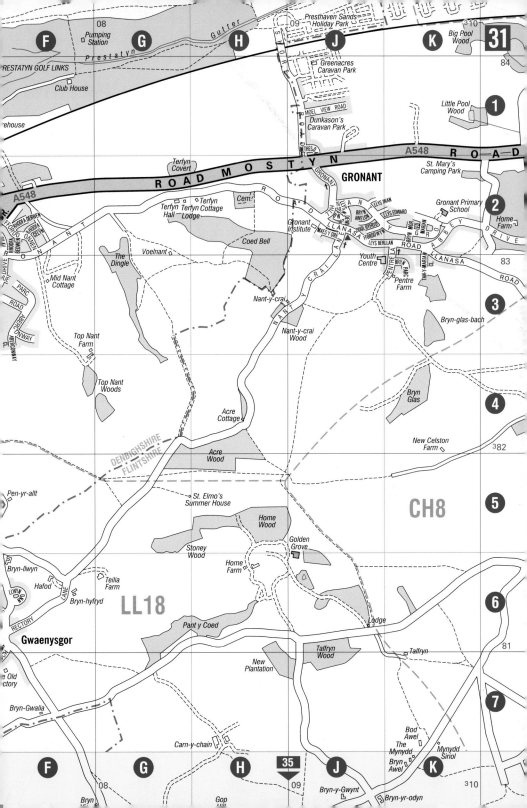

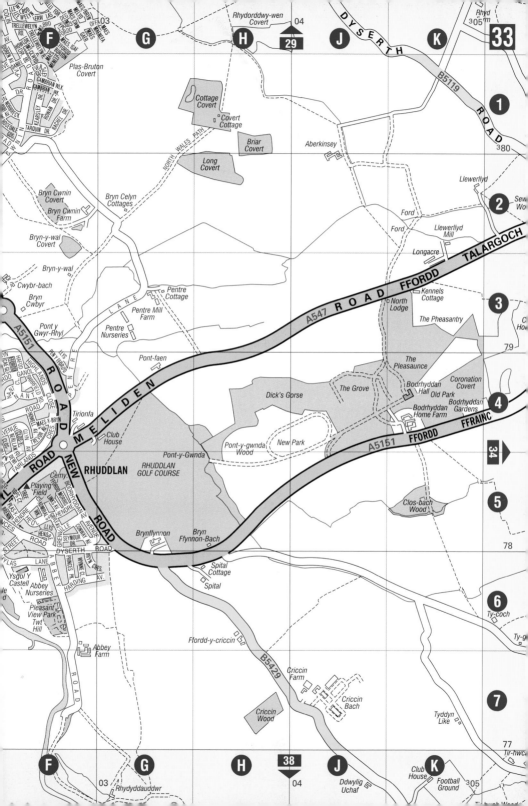

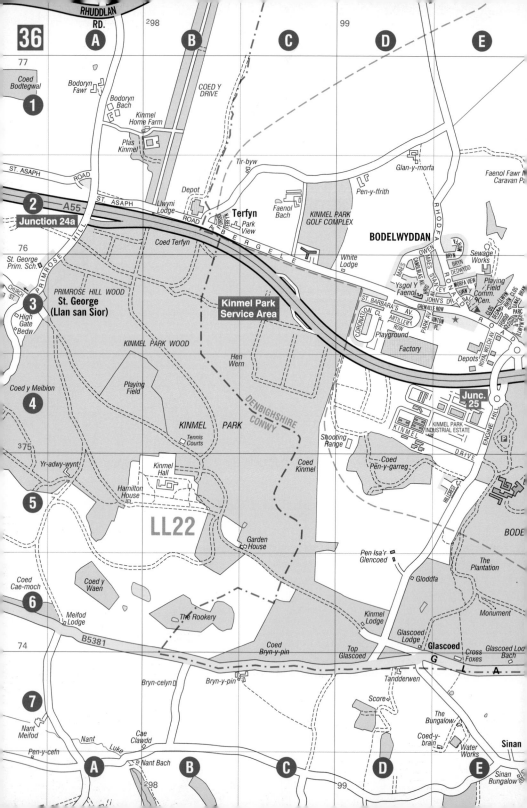

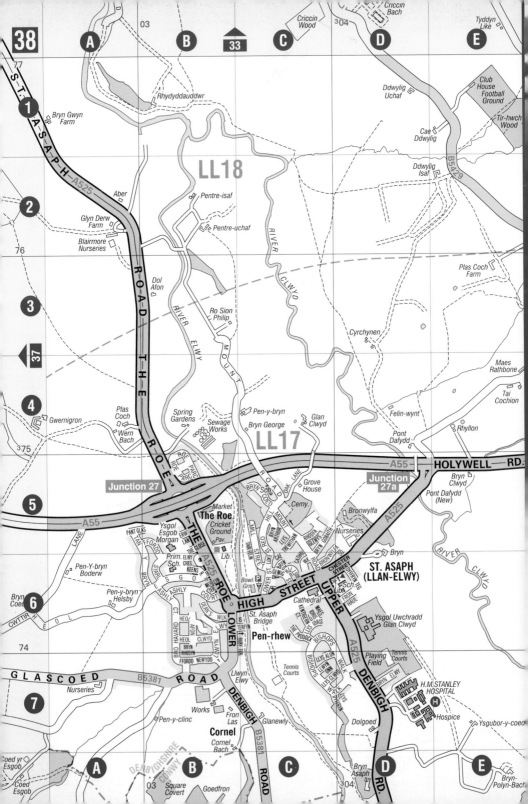

INDEX *Mynegai*

Including Streets, Industrial Estates and Selected Subsidiary Addresses.
Gan gynnwys Strydoedd, Stadau Diwydiannol a Chyfeiriadau Atodol Dethol

HOW TO USE THIS INDEX *Sut i ddefnyddio'r mynegai hwn*

1. Each street name is followed by its Posttown or Postal Locality and then by its map reference; e.g. Abbey Ct. *L'no* . . . .3E **14** is in the Llandudno Posttown and is to be found in square 3E on page **14**. The page number being shown in bold type.
A strict alphabetical order is followed in which Av., Rd., St., etc. (though abbreviated) are read in full and as part of the street name;
e.g. Ashdown Clo. appears after Ash Ct. but before Ash Gro.

*Dilynir pob enw stryd gan ei Thref bost neu ei Lleoliad Post, ac yna ei chyfeirnod map; e.e. Mae Abbey Ct. L'no . . . .3E **14** yn Nhref bost Llandudno ac mae hi yn sgwÂr 3E ar dudalen **14**. Mae rhif y dudalen wedi ei nodi mewn teip tywyll.*
Glynir yn gaeth wrth drefn a wyddor, gyda Av., Rd., St., ayb (er eu bod wedi eu talfyrru) yn cael eu darllen yn llawn ac fel rhan o enw'r stryd;
e.e. mae Áshdown Clo. yn ymddangos ar Âl Ash Ct. ond cyn Ash Gro.

2. Streets and a selection of Subsidiary names not shown on the Maps, appear in the index in Italics with the thoroughfare to which it is connected shown in brackets; e.g. Alexandra Pas. L'no . . . .3G **15** (off Bodafon St.)

*Mae enwau strydoedd a detholiad o enwau atodol sydd heb eu dangos ar y Mapiau yn ymddangos yn y mynegai mewn print italig gyda'r dramwyfa gysylltiol wedi ei dangos mewn bracedi; e.e. Alexandra Pas. L'no . . . .3G **15** (off Bodafon St.)*

GENERAL ABBREVIATIONS *Talfyriadau Cyffredinol*

All : Alley	Cotts : Cottages	La : Lane	Ri : Rise
App : Approach	Ct : Court	Lit : Little	Rd : Road
Arc : Arcade	Cres : Crescent	Lwr : Lower	Shop : Shopping
Av : Avenue	Cft : Croft	Mc : Mac	S : South
Bk : Back	Dri : Drive	Mnr : Manor	Sq : Square
Boulevd : Boulevard	E : East	Mans : Mansions	Sta : Station
Bri : Bridge	Embkmt : Embankment	Mkt : Market	St : Street
B'way : Broadway	Est : Estate	Mdw : Meadow	Ter : Terrace
Bldgs : Buildings	Fld : Field	M : Mews	Trad : Trading
Bus : Business	Gdns : Gardens	Mt : Mount	Up : Upper
Cvn : Caravan	Gth : Garth	N : North	Va : Vale
Cen : Centre	Ga : Gate	Pal : Palace	Vw : View
Chu : Church	Gt : Great	Pde : Parade	Vs : Villas
Chyd : Churchyard	Grn : Green	Pk : Park	Wlk : Walk
Circ : Circle	Gro : Grove	Pas : Passage	W : West
Cir : Circus	Ho : House	Pl : Place	Yd : Yard
Clo : Close	Ind : Industrial	Quad : Quadrant	
Comn : Common	Junct : Junction	Res : Residential	

POSTTOWN AND POSTAL LOCALITY ABBREVIATIONS *Talfyriadau Trefi Post a Lleoliadau Post*

Aber : Abergele	*Glan* : Glanwydden	*L'hos* : Llanrhos	*Rhu* : Rhuallt
Ban : Bangor	*Glyn* : Glyngarth	*L'wrn* : Llansadwrn	*Rhud* : Rhuddlan
Beau : Beaumaris	*Gron* : Gronant	*L'faen* : Llysfaen	*Rhyd* : Rhyd-y-foel
Bod : Bodelwyddan	*Gwae* : Gwaenysgor	*Maes* : Maesgeirchen	*Rhyl* : Rhyl
Bron : Bron Y Nant	*Gyf* : Gyffin	*Men B* : Menai Bridge	*St As* : St Asaph
Bryn N : Bryn Newydd	*Kin B* : Kinmel Bay	*Moch* : Mochdre	*St G* : St George
Cae : Caeathro	*L'las* : Llanddulas	*Old C* : Old Colwyn	*Star* : Star
C'fon : Caernarfon	*L'fan* : Llandegfan	*P'awr* : Penmaenmawr	*T'bont* : Talybont
Col B : Colwyn Bay	*L'no* : Llandudno	*P'edd* : Penrhosgarnedd	*Tal* : Tal-y-bont
Con : Conwy	*Llan J* : Llandudno Junction	*Pen B* : Penrhyn Bay	*Tan* : Tan-y-lan
Deg : Deganwy	*L'gai* : Llandygai	*P'side* : Penrhynside	*Tow* : Towyn
D'chi : Dwygyfylchi	*Llane* : Llanelian	*Pens* : Pensarn	*Tre* : Treborth
Dys : Dyserth	*L'chan* : Llanfairfechan	*Pres* : Prestatyn	*Trel* : Trelawnyd
Gaer : Gaerwen	*L'yll* : Llanfairpwllgwyngyll	*Rho* : Rhosdodrual	*Tre I* : Tremarl Ind. Est.
Gla C : Glan Conwy	*L'nin* : Llangwstenin	*R Sea* : Rhos On Sea	

A

	Aber Rd. *L'chan* 6A **12**	Alexandra Rd. *Aber* 5J **25**
	Aber Rd. *Pres* 2D **30**	Alexandra Rd. *Col B* 2J **21**
	Adele Av. *Pres* 3K **29**	Alexandra Rd. *L'no* 5F **15**
Abbey Ct. *L'no* 3E **14**	Adelphi St. *L'no* 3H **15**	Alexandra Rd. *Rhyl* 4C **28**
Abbey Dri. *Gron* 2K **31**	Admiral's Wlk. *Rhud* 5F **33**	Alice Gdns. *L'no* 5J **15**
Abbey Dri. *R Sea* 5H **17**	Ael y Broch. *Col B* 4K **21**	Allanson Rd. *R Sea* 7H **17**
Abbey Gro. *R Sea* 5H **17**	Ael-y-Bryn. *L'no* 3B **16**	Allerton Ct. *Deg* 3H **19**
Abbey Pl. *L'no* 3E **14**	Ael-y-Bryn Rd. *Col B* 3K **21**	All Saints Av. *Deg* 3G **19**
Abbey Rd. *Ban* 3D **10**	Ael-y-Garth. *C'fon* 3D **4**	Allt Cadnant. *C'fon* 4D **4**
Abbey Rd. *L'no* 3D **14**	Agnes Gro. *Col B* 3A **22**	Allt Cichle. *L'fan* 7A **6**
Abbey Rd. *R Sea* 5H **17**	Ala Las. *C'fon* 2D **4**	Allt Dewi. *Ban* 4C **10**
Abbey Rd. *Rhud* 6F **33**	Ainon Clo. *Ban* 4C **10**	Allt Glanrafon. *Ban* 2D **10**
Abbey St. *Rhyl* 6A **28**	Albert Dri. *Deg* 4H **19**	Allt Goch Bk. *Beau* 3G **7**
Aber Clwyd. *Kin B* 1J **27**	Albert Dri. Gdns. *Deg* 3J **19**	Allt Goch Fawr. *Beau* 1F **7**
Aberconwy Clo. *Pres* 3F **31**	Albert Gdns. *L'no* 5J **15**	Allt Pafiliwn. *C'fon* 4D **4**
Aberconwy Rd. *Pres* 3E **30**	Albert Pl. *Col B* 3A **22**	Alltwen. *L'faen* 5K **23**
Aberconwy Holiday Home &	Albert Rd. *Old C* 3D **22**	Allt-y-Castell. *C'fon* 4C **4**
Leisure Pk. *Con* 3C **18**	Albert St. *L'no* 3G **15**	Allt-y-Coed. *Con* 7F **19**
Aber Ct. *Pres* 5A **30**	Albert St. *Rhyl* 6C **28**	Allt y Graig. *Dys* 1B **34**
Aber Dri. *L'no* 3B **16**	Albion St. *L'no* 3G **15**	Alma St. *Beau* 2J **7**
Abergavenny Rd. *L'no* 3E **14**	Aled Av. *Rhyl* 7C **28**	Alpine Rd. *Old C* 5E **22**
Abergele Rd. *Col B & Old C*	Aled Ct. *Aber* 4J **25**	Alwen Dri. *R Sea* 7F **17**
. . . . .3K **21**	Aled Dri. *R Sea* 7G **17**	Anglesey Rd. *L'no* 2E **14**
(in two parts)	Aled Gdns. *Kin B* 2G **27**	Aquarium Cres. *Rhyl* 6A **28**
Abergele Rd. *L'las* 7K **22**	Alexanders Way. *Kin B* 2J **27**	Aquarium St. *Rhyl* 6A **28**
(Rhuddlan Rd.)	Alexandra Dri. *Pres* 5A **30**	Archers Grn. *Pres* 3A **30**
Abergele Rd. *L'las & Bod* . . .2B **36**	Alexandra Pk. *P'awr* 2K **13**	Ardre Clo. *P'awr* 2J **13**
(St Asaph Rd.)	Alexandra Pas. *L'no* 3G **15**	Arfon Av. *Pres* 4H **29**
Aber Pl. *L'no* 3B **16**	(off Bodafon St.)	Arfon Gro. *Rhyl* 7B **28**

Arfryn. *L'no* 7G **15**
Argoed. *Kin B* 4H **27**
Argoed Flats. *L'chan* 5B **12**
Argyll Rd. *L'no* 4H **15**
Arnold Clo. *Beau* 1J **7**
Arnold Gdns. *Kin B* 2G **27**
Arran Dri. *Rhyl* 1D **32**
Arran Rd. *R Sea* 1G **21**
Artillery Row. *Bod* 3D **36**
Arvon Av. *L'no* 2F **15**
Arvonia Pas. *L'no* 3F **15**
Ascot Dri. *Rhyl* 1D **32**
Ash Ct. *Rhyl* 6E **28**
Ashdown Clo. *Col B* 5H **21**
Ash Gro. *Kin B* 2H **27**
Ash Gro. *Pres* 3D **30**
Ashley Rd. *Ban* 2E **10**
Ashly Ct. *St As* 6B **38**
Aspen Gro. *Kin B* 2H **27**
Aspen Wlk. *Rhyl* 5F **29**
Assheton Ter. *C'fon* 5D **4**
(off Henwalia)
Astley Ct. *Kin B* 1H **27**
Augusta St. *L'no* 3G **15**
Avallon Av. *Llan J* 5K **19**
Avenue, The. *Bryn N* 3E **30**
Avenue, The. *Pres* 4D **30**
Avondale Dri. *Rhyl* 6F **29**
Awelon. *Tow* 4F **27**

Awelon Mor—Cae Rhos

Awelon Mor. Pres 2B 30
Awel-y-Mor. R Sea 7H 17

B

Bk. Bay View Rd. Col B 3A 22
Bk. Belgrave Rd. Col B 3A 22
Bk. Bod-Hyfryd Rd. L'no 2F 15 (off Bod-Hyfryd Rd.)
Bk. Charlton St. L'no 3G 15
Bk. East Pde. L'no 3J 15
Bk. Madoc St. L'no 3G 15
Bk. McKinley Rd. Llan J 5K 19 (off McKinley Rd.)
Bk. Regent St. Ban 2D 10
Bk. South Pde. L'no 2G 15 (off South Parade)
Bk. Station Rd. Old C 4E 22
Bk. York Rd. Deg 2F 19
Balaclava Rd. C'fon 3C 4
Balfour Rd. L'no 4J 15
Balmoral Gro. Rhyl 1K 27
Banastre Av. Pres 3C 30
Bangor Cres. Pres 4B 30
Barkby Av. Pres 1D 30
Barrfield Rd. Rhud 4F 33
Barry Rd. N. Rhyl 7A 28
Barry Rd. S. Rhyl 7A 28
Bastion Clo. Pres 1C 30
Bastion Gdns. Pres 2C 30
Bastion Rd. Pres 1C 30
Bath St. Rhyl 5B 28
Bay Vw. Rd. Col B 3A 22
Beach Av. Col B 3C 22
Beach Av. Pres 1D 30
Beach Clo. Pres 1C 30
Beach Dri. Pen B 4E 16
Beach Ho. Rd. L'las 4D 24
Beach Rd. Deg 2F 19
Beach Rd. L'las 3B 24
Beach Rd. Old C 4D 22
Beach Rd. P'awr 1J 13
Beach Rd. E. Pres 1C 30
Beach Rd. W. Pres 1B 30
Beacons Way. Con 3E 18
Beal Av. Col B 5B 22
Beaumaris Dri. L'no 5H 15
Bedford St. Rhyl 6B 28
Beech Av. Rhyl 5D 28
Beechmere Ri. Moch 3F 21
Beech Mt. Col B 3A 22
Beechwood Rd. Rhyl 4C 28
Bee Gdns. Aber 5J 25
Belgrave Rd. Col B 3A 22
Bell Cotts. P'awr 2J 13
Belle Vw. Ter. L'no 2E 14
Belvedere Pl. L'no 4H 15
Benarth Rd. Con 6G 19
Benarth Rd. Pen B 4E 16
Berllan. Aber 3K 25
Berllan Av. Rhud 5E 32
Berry St. Con 5G 19
Berthes Rd. Old C 4D 22
Berthglyd. Aber 7A 26
Berth-y-Glyd. Con 7F 19
Berth-y-Glyd Rd. Col B 4G 23
Berwyn Ct. R Sea 1G 21
Berwyn Cres. Kin B 1J 27
Berwyn Cres. Pres 2A 30
Berwyn Gdns. Pen B 4E 16
Bethesda St. Gron 1J 31
Betws Av. Kin B 1H 27
Beulah Av. L'las 5B 24
Bevan Av. Moch 2F 21
Beverley Dri. Pres 3A 30
Birch Gro. Pres 5D 30
Birch Gro. Rhyl 5E 28
Birkdale Av. Col B 4J 21
Birkdale Clo. Col B 4J 21
Bishops Quarry Rd. L'no 1D 14
Bishops Wlk. St As 7C 38
Bishopswood Rd. Pres 6D 30
Blackmarsh Rd. Moch 4E 20
Blaen Cwm. L'no 5G 15
Blaen-y-Wawr. Ban 5B 10
Bodafon Rd. L'no 4A 16
Bodafon St. L'no 3G 15
Bodannerch Dri. Rhyl 5C 28
Bodelwyddan Av. Kin B 2J 27
Bodelwydden Av. Old C 4E 22
Bodfor St. Rhyl 6B 28
Bod-Hyfryd Rd. L'no 2F 15
Bod Llewelyn. Rhyl 7F 29
Bodlondeb Hill. L'no 2F 15
Bodnant Av. Pres 2E 30
Bodnant Cres. L'no 5H 15
Bodnant Rd. L'no 5H 15
Bodnant Rd. R Sea 1F 21
Bodowen Ter. Men B 3K 9
Bodrhyddan Av. Rhud 5F 33
Bosworth Gro. Pres 3E 30
Boulevard, The. Pres 4J 29
Boulevd, The. Rhyl 1E 32
Brackley Av. Col B 2J 21
Brae, The. Pres 7C 30
Breton St. L'no 3F 15
Brettenham Rd. R Sea 1H 21
Brewis Rd. R Sea 6G 17
Brick St. Ban 2E 10
Bridgegate Rd. Rhyl 5D 28
Bridge Ind. Est. Rhyl 7B 28
Bridge Rd. L'no 5F 15
Bridge Rd. Pres 2C 30
Bridge St. Aber 5K 25
Bridge St. Rhyl 7A 28
Brighton Rd. Rhyl 6B 28
Brig-y-Don. L'las 4A 24
Brig-y-Don. Pres 3J 29
Britannia Sq. Ban 2D 10
Broad St. Llan J 4J 19
Broadway. Pres 4A 30
Broadway. R Sea 1H 21
Broadway Ct. Aber 5J 25 (off Broadway, The)
Broadway, The. Aber 6J 25
Bro Dawel. Men B 1H 9
Bro Deg. Rhyl 7F 29
Bro Emrys. T'bont 5J 11 (in two parts)
Bro Havard. St As 7B 38
Bro Helen. C'fon 5D 4
Bro Hyfryd. Men B 2J 9
Bro Llewelyn. L'fan 5A 6
Bro Madog. Llane 6D 22
Brompton Av. R Sea 7H 17
Brompton Pk. R Sea 7G 17
Bron Deg. Dys 4B 34
Bron Fedw. Men B 2K 9
Bron Gele. Aber 5B 26
Bron Haul. Dys 3C 34
Bron Haul. L'fan 6B 6
Bron Haul. Rhyl 6F 29
Bron Haul. Trel 2H 35
Bron Llyn. L'las 4A 24
Bron Vardre Av. Deg 3G 19
Bronwen Av. Kin B 2H 27
Bron Wern. L'las 4A 24
Bronwylfa Sq. St As 6C 38
Bron-y-De. Ban 5B 10
Bron-y-Felin. L'fan 6B 6
Bron-y-Gaer. Deg 2H 19
Bron-y-Garth. C'fon 3D 4
Bron-y-Llan. L'faen 6J 23
Bron-y-Llan Rd. L'faen 6J 23
Bron-y-Nant Rd. Bron 2F 21
Bron yr Afon. Con 6F 19
Bro Ogwen. Ban 6K 9
Brookdale Rd. Rhyl 6D 28
Brookes Av. Rhyl 1B 32
Brookes St. L'no 3G 15
Brookfield Dri. R Sea 1F 21
Brooklands. Col B 6E 22
Brook Pk. Av. Pres 2D 30
Bro Seiont. C'fon 4F 5
Bro Seiri. Ban 1F 11 (off Stryd Ambrose)
Bryn. Ban 6H 11
Brynafon. Men B 3K 9
Bryn Afon. Rhud 4E 32
Bryn Arthur. St As 5C 38
Bryn Av. Kin B 1J 27
Bryn Av. Old C 5B 22
Bryn Av. R Sea 6H 17
Bryn Av. Rhyl 5E 28
Bryn Awel. Con 7E 18
Bryn Awel Av. Aber 6K 25
Bryn Awelon. Gron 2J 31
Bryn Awelon. L'fan 7A 6
Bryn Bedw. Aber 7J 25
Bryn Benarth. Con 7G 19
Bryn Bras. L'yll 3E 8
Bryn Bras Ter. L'yll 3E 8 (off Lon Drych)
Bryn Cadno. Col B 5K 21
Bryn Castell. Aber 7J 25
Bryn Castell. Con 7F 19
Bryn Celyn. Col B 5J 21
Bryn Celyn. Con 5F 19
Bryn Celyn. L'las 4A 24
Bryn Clwyd. Aber 7J 25
Bryn Coch. Aber 6K 25
Bryn Coed. St As 5C 38
Bryn Coed Coch. Col B 5D 22
Bryn Coed Pk. Rhyl 7E 28
Bryn Coed Ter. L'chan 5C 12
Bryn Colwyn. Col B 3G 23
Bryn Ct. Pres 5B 30
Bryn Cres. Rhud 6F 33
Bryn Cwnin Rd. Rhyl 2E 32
Bryn Dedwydd. Bod 3E 36
Bryn Defaid. R Sea 7G 17
Bryn Derw. Llan J 5A 20
Bryn Derwen. Aber 7K 25
Bryn Difyr. Ban 3E 10
Bryndulas Rd. L'las 6B 24
Bryn Dymchwell. Ban 6H 11
Bryn Eglwys. Llan J 4J 19
Bryn Eglwys. R Sea 6G 17
Bryn Eirias Clo. Old C 4B 22
Bryn Eithin. Con 6G 19
Bryneithin Av. Pres 3D 30
Bryn Eithinog. Ban 4B 10
Bryn Elian Gro. Kin B 4J 27
Bryn Elwy. St As 7D 38
Bryn Eryr. Col B 5J 21
Bryn Felin. Con 7E 18
Bryn Ffynnon. Llan J 4A 20
Bryn Ffynnon. Star 2A 8
Bryn Ffynnon Ter. Old C 4D 22
Bryn Gannog. Deg 1F 19
Bryn Garan. Col B 4J 21
Bryn Gobaith. St As 6C 38
Bryn Golan. L'yll 3E 8 (off Lon Drych)
Bryn Golau. L'las 5A 24
Bryngosol Gdns. L'no 7G 15
Bryngosol Rd. L'no 7G 15
Bryn Gwelfor. Aber 7J 25
Bryn Gwyn. Aber 7J 25
Bryn Gwynt La. P'side 4C 16
Bryn Gynog Cvn. Pk. Con 7E 18
Bryn Hafod. Col B 3H 21
Bryn Hafod. Rhud 4F 33
Brynhedydd Bay. Rhyl 4F 29
Brynhedydd Rd. Rhyl 4F 29
Bryn Heli. Col B 4F 23
Bryn Helyg. Aber 7K 25
Bryn Helyg. P'awr 2K 13
Bryn Her Ter. L'las 5A 24
Bryn Heulog. Llan J 4A 20
Bryn Heulog. Old C 4E 22
Bryn Heulog Ter. Ban 5C 10
Bryn Hyfryd. C'fon 6E 4
Brynhyfryd. Dys 3A 34
Brynhyfryd Av. Rhyl 6C 28
Brynhyfryd Gro. Aber 6K 25
Bryn Hyfryd Pk. Con 5F 19
Bryn Hyfryd Ter. Con 5F 19 (off Bryn Hyfryd Pk.)
Bryniau. Pres 4E 30
Bryniau Duon. L'fan 4C 6
Bryniau Pl. L'no 5F 15
Bryniau Rd. L'no 4F 15
Bryn Ithel. Aber 7J 25
Bryn La. Beau 2J 7
Bryn Llan. Aber 7K 25
Bryn Llwyd. Ban 5B 10 (in two parts)
Bryn Llwyd Bungalows. Ban 5B 10
Brynllys. Pres 7C 30
Bryn-Llys. Rhyl 6F 29
Brynllys E. Pres 7C 30
Brynllys W. Pres 7C 30
Bryn Lupus Dri. L'no 7J 15
Bryn Lupus Rd. L'no 1H 19
Bryn Maelgwyn La. L'no 1H 19
Bryn Mair. L'chan 6B 12
Bryn Mair Av. Aber 6K 25
Bryn Marl. Llan J 3J 19
Bryn-Marl Rd. Moch 3E 20
Bryn Menai. R Sea 6H 17
Bryn Mor. Gron 2K 31
Brynmor Av. Rhyl 1D 32
Bryn Mor Ct. Pen B 4D 16
Bryn Morfa. Bod 3E 36
Brynmor Ter. P'awr 2J 13
Bryn Ogwen. Ban 6K 9
Bryn Onnen. Aber 7J 25
Bryn Parc. Aber 7K 25
Bryn Parc. Gron 3K 31
Brynpydew Rd. Llan J 2B 20
Bryn Rhedyn. L'chan 6B 12
Bryn Rhos. Rho 4G 5
Bryn Rhosyn. Aber 7K 25
Bryn Rhosyn. St As 6B 38
Bryn Rhyg. Col B 5J 21
Bryn Rd. L'chan 5B 12
Bryn Rd. Tow 3E 26
Bryn Seiri. Con 7F 19
Bryn Seiriol. L'no 1G 19
Bryn-Seiri Rd. Con 7F 19
Bryn Siriol. L'las 4B 24
Bryn Teg. Beau 1J 7
Bryn Teg. L'wrn 6B 6
Bryn Teg. Pres 3D 30
Bryn Teg. Tow 4F 27
Bryn Teg Av. Old C 4C 22
Bryn Teg Dri. R Sea 1H 21
Bryn Ter. Gyf 7F 19
Bryn Tirion. Beau 1J 7
Bryn Tirion. L'yll 3F 9
Bryntirion Av. Pres 4D 30
Bryntirion Av. Rhyl 5D 28
Bryntirion Ct. Pres 4D 30
Bryntirion Dri. Pres 4D 30
Bryn Tirion Pk. Con 7F 19
Bryntirion Ter. Aber 6K 25 (off Chapel St.)
Bryn Tirion Ter. Llan J 4K 19
Bryn Twr. Aber 6J 25
Bryn Vw. Rd. Pen B 5E 16
Bryn-y-Bia Clo. L'no 4B 16
Bryn-y-Bia Rd. L'no 3B 16
Bryn-y-Coed. Con 3H 19
Bryn-y-Fedwen. L'no 7G 15
Bryn y Felin. Dys 3B 34
Bryn-y-Gof. Cae 6G 5
Bryn-y-Mor Rd. Col B 1J 21
Buckley Av. Rhyl 7A 28
Builder St. L'no 4G 15
Builder St. W. L'no 5G 15
Bulkeley Cotts. Beau 1J 7
Bulkeley Ter. Beau 2K 7 (off Castle St.)
Bunkers Hill. Beau 1J 7
Burgedin Ter. Rhud 5E 32 (off Cross St.)
Burlington Cres. Rhyl 7D 28
Burlington Dri. Pres 4A 30
Burns Dri. Rhyl 4D 28
Butterton Rd. Rhyl 6A 28
Buxton Ct. Rhyl 7A 28
Bwlch Farm Rd. Deg 2H 19
Bwlch-y-Gwynt Rd. L'faen 7H 23
Bychan Av. Deg 3H 19
Byron St. Trel 2J 35

C

Cader Av. Kin B 3H 27
Cadnan Ct. Beau 1K 7
Cadnant Av. Pres 1D 30
Cadnant Pk. Con 5F 19
Cadwalader. Kin B 3J 27
Cadwgan Av. Col B 4D 22
Cadwgan Rd. Col B 4D 22
Caeau Bach. C'fon 6E 4
Cae Bach. L'no 4G 15
Cae Bach. T'bont 6J 11
Cae Berger. Men B 1J 9
Cae Berllan. C'fon 3E 4
Cae Blodau. Kin B 3H 27
Cae Bold. C'fon 3F 5
Cae Bryn. St As 6C 38
Cae Capel. Deg 2J 19
Cae Cilmelyn. Ban 6K 9
Cae Clyd. L'no 4J 15
Cae Cnyciog. L'yll 3D 8
Cae Coed. Llan J 3K 19
Cae Corn Hir. C'fon 5D 4
Cae Cyd Rd. D'chi 7H 13
Cae Derw. Llan J 5A 20
Cae Ffynnon. L'fan 4C 6
Caeffynnon Rd. L'chan 5B 12
Cae Glas. Col B 5G 23
Cae Glas Cres. P'awr 7H 13
Cae Groes. C'fon 5D 4
Cae Gruffydd. Rhyl 7F 29
Cae Gweithdy. Men B 1J 9
Cae Gwigin. T'bont 6J 11
Cae Gwyn. C'fon 2E 4
Cae Gwynan. D'chi 6J 13
Caellepa. Ban 3E 10
Cae Llwybr. C'fon 3F 5
Cae Maeslod Wig. Ban 3C 10
Cae Mair. Beau 2H 7
Cae Mair Uchaf. Beau 2H 7
Cae Mawr. L'no 5F 15
Cae Melyn. L'las 5A 24
Cae Mur. C'fon 3E 4
Cae Nicholas. Men B 1J 9
Cae'r Deon. Ban 4C 10
Caerfelin. L'fan 6B 6
Cae'r Garreg. C'fon 4E 4
Caer Gelach. Glyn 6C 6
Cae Rhos. L'no 7J 15

40 A-Z Bangor

Caer Nant. *Pres* 2D **30**
Cae'r Saint. *C'fon* 4E **4**
Caerwen Ter. *P'awr* 2H **13**
(off Rock Villa Rd.)
Cae'r Ymryson. *C'fon* 5D **4**
Cae Uchaf. *Rhyl* 5D **28**
Calthorpe Dri. *Pres* 5D **30**
Cambrian Dri. *Pres* 6D **30**
Cambrian Dri. *R Sea* 1F **21**
Cambrian Wlk. *Rhyl* 1F **33**
(in two parts)
Cambrian Way. *R Sea* 7F **17**
Cambria Rd. *Col B* 4F **23**
Campbell Clo. *Pen B* 5C **16**
Canning Rd. *Col B* 3A **22**
Canolblas Av. *Bod* 3D **36**
Canol Cruddyn. *L'no* 4H **15**
Canterbury Dri. *Pres* 4B **30**
Canterbury La. *R Sea* 6G **17**
Caradoc Rd. *Llan J* 5K **19**
Caradoc Rd. *Pres* 2D **30**
Caradog Pl. *L'chan* 4A **12**
Cardiff Way. *Pres* 5B **30**
Cardoc Ter. *St As* 6B **38**
(off Llwyn Elwy)
Carlisle Av. *Rhyl* 4E **28**
Carlton Rd. *Col B* 2J **21**
Carlton Way. *Rhyl* 1E **32**
Carmen Sylva Rd. *L'no* 3K **15**
Carolina Cres. *Pen B* 5E **16**
Caroline Rd. *L'no* 3G **15**
Carpenter Av. *L'no* 5J **15**
Carreg Felin. *L'fan* 5B **6**
Carreg Heilyn La. *Dys* 3B **34**
Carreg-y-Gad. *L'yll* 2D **8**
Carroll Pl. *L'no* 3E **14**
Castle Hill Ter. *Ban* 3E **10**
Castle Pl. *Aber* 5K **25**
Castle Row. *Beau* 1J **7**
Castle Sq. *Con* 5G **19**
Castle St. *Con* 5G **19**
Castle St. *Rhud* 5E **32**
Castle Vw. Ter. *Ban* 7E **6**
Cathedral Wlk. *St As* 6C **38**
Catherine Av. *Pres* 3K **29**
Cayley Promenade.
R Sea 7J **17**
Cedar Av. *Rhyl* 6E **28**
Cedar Gro. *R Sea* 7G **17**
Cedar Pk. *Col B* 4H **21**
Cefn Cadnant. *C'fon* 4E **4**
Cefndy Rd. *Rhyl* 1B **32**
Cefndy Rd. Employment Pk. *Rhyl*
. . . . .1C **32**
Cefndy Trad. Est. *Rhyl* 7C **28**
Cefn Hendre. *C'fon* 5D **4**
Cefn Menai. *C'fon* 3D **4**
Cefn Rd. *Old C* 4D **22**
Cefn Talar. *C'fon* 4D **4**
Cefn-y-Bryn. *L'no* 7G **15**
Cefn y Gwrych. *Pres* 6C **30**
Ceg-y-Ffordd. *Pres* 3K **29**
Cei Banc. *C'fon* 4C **4**
Cei Llechi. *C'fon* 4C **4**
(in two parts)
Ceiswyn Pl. *Pres* 3D **30**
Celyn Av. *P'awr* 2J **13**
Celyn St. *P'awr* 2J **13**
Cemlyn Clo. *P'awr* 1K **13**
Cemlyn Pk. *P'awr* 1K **13**
Central Av. *Pres* 3C **30**
Central Pl. *L'no* 4G **15**
Ceri Av. *Pres* 3K **29**
Chantrey Pas. *L'no* 4H **15**
(off Bodafon St.)
Chapel Rd. *Pres* 2B **30**
Chapel St. *Aber* 6K **25**
Chapel St. *Beau* 2J **7**
Chapel St. *Con* 5G **19**
Chapel St. *L'no* 3G **15**
Chapel St. *Moch* 4F **21**
Chapel St. *P'awr* 2G **13**
Chapel St. *Trel* 2J **35**
Charleston Av. *Pres* 4J **29**
Charleston Clo. *Pen B* 5D **16**
Charleston Rd. *Pen B* 5D **16**
Charlesville Rd. *Kin B* 2J **27**
Charlotte Rd. *L'no* 4H **15**
Charlton St. *L'no* 3G **15**
Chatsworth Rd. *Rhyl* 7B **28**
Cheltenham Av. *Rhyl* 6E **28**
Cherry Clo. *Pres* 4H **29**
Cherry Tree Clo. *Col B* 4H **21**
Cherry Tree La. *Col B* 3H **21**
Cherry Tree Wlk. *Rhyl* 5E **28**
Chester Av. *Kin B* 4H **27**
Chester Clo. *Pres* 4B **30**

Chester St. *Rhyl* 5C **28**
Chester St. *St As* 6D **38**
Chestnut Av. *D'chi* 6J **13**
Chestnut Ct. *Rhyl* 5E **28**
Chichester Dri. *Pres* 4B **30**
Christina Av. *Pres* 4J **29**
Church Clo. *Pen B* 5E **16**
Church Cres. *L'no* 4E **14**
Church Dri. *R Sea* 5H **17**
Churchill Clo. *Old C* 4F **23**
Church La. *Pres* 3D **30**
Church Rd. *P'awr* 1K **13**
Church Rd. *R Sea* 6G **17**
Church St. *Aber* 5K **25**
Church St. *Ban* 4C **10**
Church St. *Beau* 1J **7**
Church St. *Con* 5G **19**
Church St. *Rhud* 5E **32**
Church St. *Rhyl* 5B **28**
Church St. *St G* 3A **36**
Church Vw. *Bod* 3E **36**
(off Rhodfa Ronald)
Church Walks. *L'no* 3F **15**
Church Walks. *Old C* 4D **22**
Churton Rd. *Rhyl* 5C **28**
Cil Bedlam. *Men B* 2J **9**
Cil Coed. *Ban* 5B **10**
Cil Coed. *C'fon* 4E **4**
Cilfan. *Aber* 5A **26**
Cilfan. *Con* 7E **18**
Cilgant Alotan. *P'edd* 6K **9**
Cilgant Eglwys Wen.
Bod 3F **37**
Cilgwyn. *Llan J* 4A **20**
Cilgwyn Rd. *Llane* 7K **21**
Cil Isaf. *C'fon* 4E **4**
Cil Peblig. *C'fon* 5E **4**
Cil Uchaf. *C'fon* 4E **4**
Cil-y-Bont. *Pres* 2D **30**
Cil y Graig. *L'yll* 3E **8**
Cil-y-Graig. *Men B* 1J **9**
Circle, The. *Kin B* 2G **27**
Circle, The. *Pres* 3E **30**
Claremont Rd. *L'no* 3G **15**
Clarence Cres. *L'no* 4J **15**
Clarence Dri. *L'no* 4J **15**
Clarence Gdns. *L'no* 3J **15**
Clarence Rd. *L'no* 3J **15**
Clare Vs. *L'no* 5F **15**
Claughton Rd. *Col B* 3K **21**
Clayton Dri. *Pres* 5D **30**
Clement Av. *L'no* 3F **15**
Clement Dri. *Rhyl* 7F **29**
Clement Pl. *L'no* 3F **15**
Clement St. *L'no* 3F **15**
Cliff-Don. *Pen B* 4E **16**
Cliff Gdns. *Old C* 3E **22**
Cliff Rd. *Col B* 4D **22**
Clifton Av. *Rhyl* 6D **28**
Clifton Gro. *Rhyl* 6D **28**
Clifton Pk. Rd. *Rhyl* 6D **28**
Clifton Ri. *Aber* 6H **25**
Clifton Rd. *L'no* 3F **15**
Clifton Rd. *Old C* 3E **22**
Clipterfyn. *L'las* 5C **24**
Clive Av. *Pres* 3J **29**
Clobryn Rd. *L'faen* 4J **23**
Clonmel Pas. *L'no* 3G **15**
Clonmel St. *L'no* 3G **15**
Clos Bodnant. *Pres* 2D **30**
Clos Brenig. *Bod* 3E **36**
Clos Dinas Bran. *Bod* 3E **36**
Clos Dinbych. *Bod* 3E **36**
Close, The. *Col B* 4A **22**
Close, The. *L'chan* 5B **12**
Close, The. *Pen B* 6D **16**
Close, The. *St As* 5B **38**
Clos Fforddisa. *Pres* 4D **30**
Clos Gladstone. *Rhyl* 5D **28**
Clos Hen Felin. *D'chi* 6J **13**
Clos Morfudd. *Rhyl* 7F **29**
Clos Teg Fan. *Rhyl* 7F **29**
Clos-y-Berllan. *Rhud* 4F **33**
(in two parts)
Clos y Nant. *P'awr* 2K **13**
Clwyd Av. *Aber* 5K **25**
Clwyd Av. *Dys* 4B **34**
Clwyd Av. *Pres* 3D **30**
Clwyd Av. *Rhud* 4E **32**
Clwyd Av. *Rhyl* 7B **28**
Clwyd Bank. *Kin B* 2J **27**
Clwyd Ct. *Pres* 5A **30**
Clwyd Cres. *Con* 1G **21**
Clwyd Gdns. *Kin B* 2G **27**
Clwyd Pk. *Kin B* 4J **27**
Clwyd St. *Rhyl* 6B **28**
Coed Av. *Kin B* 5K **27**

Coed Bedw. *Aber* 6J **25**
Coed Celyn. *Aber* 6J **25**
Coed Coch Rd. *Old C* 4D **22**
Coed Eithin. *Aber* 6J **25**
Coed Gwern. *Aber* 6J **25**
Coed Llawryf. *Aber* 7J **25**
Coed Masarn. *Aber* 6J **25**
Coed Mor Dri. *Pres* 4D **30**
Coed-Pella Rd. *Col B* 3K **21**
Coed Pin. *Aber* 7J **25**
Coed y Castell. *Ban* 2G **11**
Coed-y-Glyn. *Col B* 4H **21**
Coed-y-Glyn. *L'no* 7G **15**
Coed y Maes. *P'edd* 5K **9**
Coed y Mor. *Pen B* 4D **16**
Colin Dri. *Rhyl* 7F **29**
College Av. *R Sea* 6H **17**
Collen Wen. *L'yll* 2D **8**
Colwyn Av. *R Sea* 6J **17**
Colwyn Cen., The. *Col B* 3A **22**
Colwyn Cres. *R Sea* 6H **17**
Colwyn Pl. *L'no* 3B **16**
Colwyn Rd. *L'no* 3K **15**
Combermere Rd. *Col B* 3J **21**
Compton Way. *Aber* 6K **25**
Coniston Dri. *Pres* 2B **30**
Conolly Clo. *Pen B* 5C **16**
Constitution Hill. *P'awr* 2J **13**
Conway Av. *Rhud* 5F **33**
Conway Clo. *R Sea* 7F **17**
Conway Cres. *L'no* 7G **15**
Conway Gro. *Pres* 3C **30**
Conway Rd. *Gla C* 7A **20**
Conway Rd. *L'no* 3H **15**
Conway Rd. *Llan J* 5J **19**
Conway Rd. *Moch* 2F **21**
Conway Rd. *Con* 3B **20**
Conwy St. *Rhyl* 5C **28**
Copthorn M. *Col B* 4H **21**
Copthorn Rd. *Col B* 4H **21**
Coronation Clo. *Bod* 3D **36**
Coronation Rd. *Men B* 2K **9**
Council St. W. *L'no* 4H **15**
County Dri. *Rhyl* 5D **28**
County Path. *L'no* 4H **15**
Court St. *L'no* 2G **15**
Coventry Dri. *Rhyl* 6C **28**
Coventry Gro. *Pres* 3A **30**
Cowlyd Clo. *R Sea* 7G **17**
Crafnant Rd. *R Sea* 1F **21**
Craig Dri. *Aber* 4E **16**
Craig Rd. *Old C* 3B **16**
Craigside Dri. *L'no* 3B **16**
Craig Vw. *R Sea* 7G **17**
Craig Wen. *R Sea* 7G **17**
Craig-y-Don. *Aber* 3K **25**
Craig y Don Pde. *L'no* 3K **15**
Cramer Ct. *Rhyl* 7B **28**
Cranford Cres. *R Sea* 5H **17**
Crescent Ct. *L'no* 3H **15**
Crescent Rd. *Rhyl* 6D **28**
Crescent, The. *R Sea* 5H **17**
Crescent, The. *Rhyl* 6C **28**
Criafolen. *Aber* 5B **26**
(off Towyn Rd.)
Criccieth Clo. *L'no* 5H **15**
Crimea Ter. *P'awr* 2G **13**
Crogfryn La. *L'no* 1J **19**
Cromlech Rd. *L'no* 5J **15**
Crossley Rd. *R Sea* 7H **17**
Cross St. *Rhud* 5E **32**
Crown La. *Con* 5G **19**
Crugan Av. *Kin B* 2H **27**
Cuffnell Clo. *L'no* 5J **15**
Curzon Pas. *L'no* 4J **15**
Curzon Rd. *L'no* 4J **15**
Cwlach Gdns. *L'no* 2F **15**
Cwlach Rd. *L'no* 2F **15**
Cwm Estyn. *Deg* 3J **19**
Cwm Howard La. *L'no* 6H **15**
Cwm Isaf. *L'no* 5H **15**
(off Parc Bodnant)
Cwmlws La. *P'awr* 3G **13**
Cwm Pl. *L'no* 5H **15**
Cwm Rd. *Dys* 4B **34**
Cwm Rd. *L'no* 4G **15**
Cwm Rd. *L'no* 4G **15**
Cwm Silyn. *C'fon* 6E **4**
Cwm Teg. *Old C* 5D **22**
Cwrt Bryn-y-Bia. *L'no* 4C **16**
Cwrt Cae Mor. *Tow* 4J **15**
Cwrt Dowell. *Pres* 3C **30**
Cwrt Dyffryn. *Old C* 6D **22**
Cwrt Gele. *Aber* 5B **26**
Cwrt M W Hughes. *L'no* 5J **15**
Cwrt y Coleg. *R Sea* 1J **21**
Cwrt-y-Dderwen. *Col B* 3K **21**

Cwttir La. *St As* 6K **37**
Cwymp Rd. *Rhyd* 6B **24**
Cyffordd Llandudno Ind. Est. *Llan J*
. . . . .5B **20**
Cylch Tudor. *L'no* 4H **15**
Cyll Ter. *L'no* 2E **14**
Cynfran Rd. *L'faen* 5K **23**
Cynlas. *Kin B* 4H **27**
Cypress Gro. *Rhyl* 5E **28**
Cystennin Rd. *L'nin* 3E **20**

D

Dakla Dri. *Pen B* 5E **16**
Dale Rd. *L'no* 4E **14**
Dale, The. *Aber* 6H **25**
Daniel Dri. *Rhyl* 1F **33**
Daresbury Clo. *L'no* 5J **15**
David Clo. *Pres* 4C **30**
David Edwards Clo. *Old C* 4D **22**
Davids La. *P'awr* 2J **13**
David St. *P'awr* 2J **13**
Davies' Pas. *L'no* 4G **15**
(off Norman Rd.)
Davies Way. *L'no* 4G **15**
(off Norman Rd.)
Dawson Clo. *Pres* 4C **30**
Dawson Ct. *Pres* 4C **30**
Dawson Cres. *Pres* 4C **30**
Dawson Dri. *Pres* 3C **30**
Ddol Ddu. *Old C* 6D **22**
Ddol Ddu Isaf. *Col B* 5D **22**
Ddol Hyfryd. *Gron* 2J **31**
Dean's Wlk. *St As* 6B **38**
Deganwy Av. *L'no* 3F **15**
Deganwy Beach. *Deg* 1F **19**
Deganwy Rd. *L'hos* 7F **15**
Dell, The. *Pres* 4C **30**
Denbigh Circ. *Kin B* 4J **27**
Denmore Av. *Rhyl* 4E **28**
Denness Pl. *L'no* 4F **15**
Derby Ter. *Aber* 5J **25**
Derrie Av. *Aber* 5H **25**
Derwen Av. *R Sea* 1F **21**
Derwen Dri. *Rhyl* 2E **32**
Derwen La. *L'no & Pen B* 5C **16**
Derwen Las. *C'fon* 6E **4**
Derwen Rd. *Pen B* 6D **16**
Derwen Rd. *P'awr* 2G **13**
Derwent Clo. *Pres* 2B **30**
Deva Clo. *R Sea* 7G **17**
Deva Cres. *Rhyl* 5D **28**
Dew St. *Men B* 2K **9**
Diane Dri. *Rhyl* 1D **32**
Digby Rd. *R Sea* 7H **17**
Dinas Av. *Kin B* 2G **27**
Dinas Rd. *L'no* 4F **15**
Dinerth Av. *R Sea* 6F **17**
Dinerth Clo. *R Sea* 6F **17**
Dinerth Cres. *R Sea* 6F **17**
Dinerth Hall Rd. *R Sea* 6F **17**
Dinerth Pk. *R Sea* 6G **17**
Dinerth Rd. *R Sea* 7F **17**
Dingle Hill. *Col B* 4A **22**
Dingle, The. *Col B* 3A **22**
Dock Rd. *C'fon* 3C **4**
Doctor Garretts Dri. *Con* 4E **18**
Dodgson Clo. *L'no* 5J **15**
Dol Acar. *Rhyd* 7C **24**
Dol Dderw. *Llan J* 5A **20**
Dol Eithin. *Pen B* 4E **16**
Dol Elian. *Old C* 5D **22**
Dol Goed. *Llan J* 4K **19**
Dol-Helyg. *T'bont* 6J **11**
Dol Hudol. *Llan J* 3J **19**
Dolphin Ct. *R Sea* 1G **21**
Dolwen Clo. *L'faen* 7J **23**
Dolwen Rd. *L'faen* 7H **23**
Dolwen Rd. *Old C* 6E **22**
Dol Wynne. *L'las* 4A **24**
Dolydd. *L'no* 4F **15**
Dolydd. *Llan J* 4K **19**
Donald Av. *Rhyl* 1D **32**
Dorchester Clo. *Rhyl* 2E **32**
Doren Av. *Rhyl* 7F **29**
Douglas Rd. *Col B* 3A **22**
Drake Clo. *Pen B* 4E **16**
Drummond Pas. *L'no* 3G **15**
Duchess Clo. *L'no* 5J **15**
Dulas Av. *Kin B* 3H **27**
Dulas Clo. *R Sea* 7G **17**
Dulas Rd. *Kin B* 3H **27**
Dundonald Av. *Aber* 5K **25**
Dundonald Rd. *Col B* 4A **22**
Durham Dri. *Pres* 4B **30**
Durleston Dri. *Pres* 4A **30**

Durrant Clo.—Gilfach Rd.

Durrant Clo. Rhyl 1E 32
Dwyfor Ct. Pres 5A 30
Dwyrain Twthill. C'fon 4D 4
Dyffryn Rd. L'no 4F 15
Dyffryn Teg. Rhu 6D 38
Dyserth Rd. Rhud 6F 33
Dyserth Rd. Rhyl 6E 28
Dyserth Rd. Trel 3C 34

E

Eagles Farm Rd. Moch 4E 20
Earlswood Av. Pres 3J 29
East Av. Pres 3E 30
East Clo. Pres 3H 29
East Pde. L'no 3J 15
East Pde. Rhyl 5B 28
Eastville Av. Rhyl 4E 28
Eaton Av. Old C 4C 22
Eaton Av. Rhyl 4E 28
Ebberston Rd. E. R Sea 1H 21
Ebberston Rd. W. R Sea 1H 21
Eden Av. Pres 3D 30
Edgbaston Rd. Rhyl 5F 29
Edge Hill. Ban 7E 6
Edward Henry St. Rhyl 6A 28
Edwards St. L'no 3G 15
Edward St. P'awr 2H 13
Egerton Rd. Col B 2J 21
Eirian Av. Kin B 3J 27
Eirias Rd. Col B 4B 22
Elan Rd. L'no 5H 15
Eldon Dri. Aber 5H 25
Eleanor Rd. Old C 3D 22
Eleri Clo. Rhyl 1D 32
Elfod. Aber 4K 25
Elian Rd. Col B 4B 22
Elizabeth Vs. L'no 5F 15
Ellesmere Rd. Col B 2K 21
Ellis Av. Old C 4G 23
Ellis Av. Rhyl 7A 28
Ellis Way. Con 3E 18
Elm Gro. Rhyl 5D 28
Elmsway Dri. Pres 4D 30
Elwy Av. Dys 5B 34
Elwy Circ. Kin B 3J 27
Elwy Cres. St As 6B 38
Elwy Dri. Rhyl 6C 28
Elwy Gdns. L'no 5J 15
Elwy Pl. St As . . . . 6C 38 (off Luke St.)
Elwy Rd. R Sea 6H 17
Elwy St. Rhyl 6B 28
Elwy Ter. St As . . . . 6C 38 (off Luke St.)
Elwy Vw. St As . . . . 6C 38 (off Mill St.)
Emery Down. L'no 5J 15
Emlyn Gro. Rhyl 6A 28
Endsleigh Rd. Old C 4E 22
Engine Hill. Bod 4E 36
Epworth Rd. Rhyl 2E 32
Erasmus St. P'awr 2J 13
Erddig Clo. L'no 6H 15
Ernestine Vs. L'no 5F 15
Ernest St. Rhyl 6C 28
Erskine Rd. Col B 3A 22
Erskine Ter. Con 5G 19
Erw Goch. Aber 6K 25
Erw Lan. St As 5B 38
Erw Las. Rhyl 7F 29
Erw Wen. Cae 6G 5
Erw Wen. L'las 4A 24
Erw Wen. Trel 2H 35
Erw-Wen Rd. Col B 3A 22
Eryl Pl. L'no 4F 15
Esgyryn Rd. Llan J 3A 20
Esplanade. P'awr 2H 13
Eton Pk. Rhud 5E 32
Everard Rd. R Sea 7J 17
Eversley Clo. Rhyl 1F 33
Ewloe Dri. L'no 6H 15
Exell Rd. R Sea 7H 17
Exeter Clo. Pres 3A 30

F

Faenol Av. Aber 5K 25
Fairfield Av. Rhyl 5C 28
Fairfield Clo. Pen B 5D 16
Fairlands Cres. Rhud 5F 33
Fair Mt. Old C 4D 22
Fairview. Men B 2K 9
Fairview Av. Pres 4C 30
Fairview Cres. Pres 4C 30
Fairway. R Sea 6H 17
Fairways. L'no 5F 15
Fairy Glen. Old C 4D 22
Fairy Glen Rd. P'awr 7K 13
Farrington Ct. Pen B 5C 16
Feol Vw. Rd. Rhyl 7E 28
Ferguson Av. Pres 2K 29
Fern Av. Pres 3D 30
Fernbrook Rd. P'awr 2J 13
Fern Clo. Rhyl 5F 29
Ferndale Rd. Llan J 4J 19
Fern Wlk. Rhyl 5E 28
Fern Way. Rhyl 5E 28
Ferry Farm Rd. Llan J 5H 19
Fferm Bach Rd. L'no 5K 15
Fferm La. L'no 5J 15
Ffordd Aber. Rhud 4E 32
Ffordd Ainon. Ban 4C 10
Ffordd Angharad. L'yll 3D 8
Ffordd Anwyl. Rhyl 6E 28
Ffordd Bangor. C'fon 2E 4
Ffordd Bangor. Con 4A 18
Ffordd Bangor. D'chi 6G 13
Ffordd Bangor. L'chan 3C 12
Ffordd Bangor. P'awr 2G 13
Ffordd Beaumaris. Men B 1A 10
Ffordd Belmont. Ban 3A 10
Ffordd Bethel. C'fon 3E 4
Ffordd Bont Saint. C'fon 7D 4
Ffordd Bronwydd. Tre 6H 9
Ffordd Bryniau. Pres 7C 30
Ffordd Bryn Melyd. Pres 6C 30
Ffordd Brynsiencyn. L'yll 7A 8
Ffordd Bugail. Col B 5B 22
Ffordd Burton. Rhyl 7F 29
Ffordd Bwclae. Ban 1D 10
Ffordd Cadnant. Men B 2K 9
Ffordd Cae Garw. Rho 4G 5
Ffordd Cae Glas. Rhud 4F 33
Ffordd Caergybi. Ban 4K 9
Ffordd Caergybi. Gaer & L'yll 3A 8
Ffordd Caernarfon. Ban 7A 10
Ffordd Cambria. Men B 3K 9
Ffordd Ceiriog. Ban 2E 10
Ffordd Celyn. Col B 5B 22
Ffordd Cibyn. C'fon 4F 5
Ffordd Coed Helen. C'fon 4C 4
Ffordd Coed Marion. C'fon 4F 5
Ffordd Coed Mawr. Ban 5B 10
Ffordd Conwy. P'awr 2K 13
Ffordd Craiglun. Kin B 4K 27
Ffordd Craig y Don. Ban 2D 10
Ffordd Crwys. Ban 7J 9
Ffordd Cwellyn. C'fon 3E 4
Ffordd Cwm. P'awr 2J 13
Ffordd Cwstenin. C'fon 5D 4
Ffordd Cwstenin. Moch 3F 21
Ffordd Cynan. Ban 6J 9
Ffordd Cynan. Men B 2K 9
Ffordd Cynfal. Ban 3C 10
Ffordd Dawel. Col B 5B 22
Ffordd Deiniol. Ban 3D 10
Ffordd Denman. Ban 4C 10
Ffordd Derwen. Rhyl 1C 32
Ffordd Dewi. L'no 4H 15
Ffordd Dewi. Rhud 5F 33
Ffordd Dinas. L'chan 6C 12
Ffordd Dulyn. L'no 5F 15
Ffordd Dwyfor. L'no 5H 15
Ffordd Dyffryn. Moch 2F 21
Ffordd Eithinog. Ban 4A 10
Ffordd Elan. Rhyl 5F 29
Ffordd Elfed. Ban 4F 11
Ffordd Elias. Col B 4G 23
Ffordd Elidir. C'fon 3E 4
Ffordd Elisabeth. L'no 5G 15
Ffordd Emrys. Aber 6H 25
Ffordd Eryr. Moch 3F 21
Ffordd Eryri. C'fon 5E 4
Ffordd Euryn. Moch 3F 21
Ffordd Euston. Ban 3C 10
Ffordd Farrar. Ban 3D 10
Ffordd Felin Seiont. C'fon 6D 4
Ffordd Ffriddoedd. Ban 3B 10
Ffordd Ffynnon. Dys 5B 34
Ffordd Ffynnon. Pres 5A 30
Ffordd Ffynnon. Rhud 4E 32
Ffordd Ganol. Rhud 4E 32
Ffordd Gth. Ban 2E 10
Ffordd Gth. Uchaf. Ban 1E 10
Ffordd Gelli Morgan. Ban 7G 9
Ffordd Glascoed. C'fon 3F 5
Ffordd Glynne. Ban 1E 10
Ffordd Gobaith. Moch 2F 21
Ffordd Gorad. Ban 1C 10
Ffordd Gwelfryn. Aber 5A 26
Ffordd Gwenllian. L'yll 3D 8
Ffordd Gwilym. Pres 7B 30
Ffordd Gwyndy. P'edd 6K 9
Ffordd Gwynedd. Ban 2E 10
Ffordd Gwynedd. L'no 4H 15
Ffordd Hafryn. Col B 5B 22
Ffordd Helyg. P'awr 2J 13
Ffordd Hendre. Ban 5B 10
Ffordd Hendrewen. Ban 4C 10
Ffordd Hwfa. Ban 2D 10
Ffordd Idwal. Aber 7H 25
Ffordd Isaf. Col B 3G 21
Ffordd Islwyn. Ban 1E 10
Ffordd Landygai. Ban 2G 11
Ffordd Las. L'no 4H 15
Fforddlas. Pres 3D 30
Ffordd Las. Rhyl 7B 28
Ffordd Llanbeblig. C'fon 5E 4
Ffordd Llanberis. C'fon 4E 4
Ffordd Llyn Goch. Gwae 7E 30
Ffordd Maelgwn. Tre I 5K 19
Ffordd Maes Barcer. C'fon 4E 4
Ffordd Marchlyn. C'fon 3E 4
Ffordd Marian. Gron 2K 31
Ffordd Meigan. Beau 1J 7
Ffordd Meirion. Ban 1D 10
Ffordd Menai. Ban 5K 9
Ffordd Menai. C'fon 2E 4
Ffordd Mona. Men B 2J 9
Ffordd Morfa. L'no 4H 15
Ffordd Morris. Rhud 5F 33
Ffordd Mynach. Moch 3E 20
Ffordd Nant. Kin B 4K 27
Ffordd Nant. Rhud 4E 32
Ffordd Newydd. St As 7B 38
Ffordd Offa. Rhyl 7F 29
Ffordd Onnen. Pres 2F 31
Ffordd Pafiliwn. C'fon 4D 4
Ffordd Pandy. C'fon 4F 5
Ffordd Pandy. Col B 4B 22
Ffordd Pant. C'fon 7C 4
Ffordd Pantycelyn. Pres 5A 30
Ffordd Parc Bodnant. Pres 2D 30
Ffordd Parc Castell. Bod 3E 36
Ffordd Penchwintan. Ban 4B 10
Ffordd Penclip. Men B 2K 9
Ffordd Pendyffryn. Pres 3C 30
Ffordd Penlan. Ban 7G 9
Ffordd Penmynydd. L'yll 3D 8
Ffordd Pennant. Pres 7B 30
Ffordd Penrhos. P'edd 7H 9
Ffordd Penrhwylfa. Pres 3A 30
Ffordd Penrhyn. L'no 4H 15
Ffordd Pentraeth. Men B 1H 9
Ffordd Pen y Bryn. Ban 2F 11
Ffordd Penybryn. C'fon 7D 4
Ffordd Penyffridd. Ban 5A 10
Ffordd Rhiannon. L'yll 3D 8
Ffordd Sackville. Ban 3D 10
Ffordd Sam Pari. Con 4C 18
Ffordd Santes Helen. C'fon 4C 4
Ffordd Segontiwm. C'fon 5D 4
Ffordd Seiriol. P'awr 2J 13
Ffordd Siarl. St As 5B 38
Ffordd Siglen. Col B 4B 22
Ffordd Siliwen. Ban 2D 10
Ffordd Talargoch. Dys 3K 33
Ffordd Talargoch. Pres 7C 30
Ffordd Tan'r Allt. Aber 6H 25
Ffordd Tanrallt. Pres 7C 30
Ffordd Tan y Bryn. Ban 2F 11
Ffordd Tegai. Ban 3F 11
Ffordd Tegid. Ban 2E 10
Ffordd Teifion. L'yll 2E 8
Ffordd Telford. Men B 3K 9
Ffordd Terfyn. Bod 2B 36
Ffordd Tirionfa. Col B 4E 22
Ffordd Treborth. Ban 6J 9
Ffordd Trem Deg. Ban 1F 11
Ffordd Triban. Col B 4H 21
Ffordd Tudno. L'no 4H 15
Ffordd Tyn Clwt. Ban 6K 9
Ffordd ty Newydd. Pres 7B 30
Ffordd Tysilio. Men B 2J 9
Ffordd Uchaf. Col B 3G 21
Ffordd Victoria. C'fon 4D 4
Ffordd Waunfawr. Cae 5F 5
Ffordd Wern. C'fon 4F 5
Ffordd Wyn. Gron 2J 31
Ffordd-y-Berllan. Tow 5F 27
Ffordd-y-Bryn. Moch 2F 21
Ffordd y Castell. Ban 3F 11
Ffordd y Coleg. Ban 2D 10
Ffordd y Coleg. Men B 2K 9
Ffordd y Fair. Men B 2K 9
Ffordd-y-Fedwen. Col B 5B 22
Ffordd y Fynnon. Ban 2E 10
Ffordd y Gogledd. C'fon 3D 4
Ffordd y Graig. L'las 4A 24
Ffordd-y-Graig Old C 4G 23
Ffordd-y-Llan. L'faen 5H 23
Ffordd y Llyn. Ban 7G 9
Ffordd-y-Maer. Moch 3F 21
Ffordd y Morfa Aber 4K 25
Ffordd y Paced. Men B 3K 9
Ffordd y Parc. Ban 6G 9
Ffordd-y-Pentre. Bryn P 2B 20
Ffordd y Plas. Ban 7G 9
Ffordd yr Aber. C'fon 5A 4
Ffordd yr Orsaf. Ban 3D 10
Ffordd yr Orsedd. L'no 5G 15
Ffordd Ysgubor Goch. C'fon 4E 4
Ffordd y Tywysog. Ban 2D 10
Fforrd Ffrith. Pres 3B 30
Ffrith Rd. Bryn P 2A 20
Ffynnongroew Rd. Rhyl 6B 28
Ffynnon Sadwrn La. L'no 3A 16
Field St. Ban 2C 10
First Av. Pres 1B 30
First Av. R Sea 6G 17
Foel Ct. Dys 4B 34
Foel Pk. Dys 4B 34
Foel Rd. Dys 3C 34
Foreshore Pk. R Sea 5H 17
Foryd Rd. Kin B 2G 27
Four Crosses. Tre 6H 9
Frances Av. Rhyl 1D 32
Francis Av. R Sea 1H 21
Franklyn Av. Pres 4H 29
Frank Vs. L'no 5F 15
Frederick St. Rhyl 7A 28
Friars Av. Ban 2F 11
Friar's Rd. Ban 2F 11
Fron Cres. L'chan 6C 12
Fron Deg. L'fan 6B 6
Frondeg. L'yll 2E 8
Fron Deg Rd. P'side 5C 16
Fron Farm. Men B 1H 9
Fron Haul. St As 6D 38
Fron Heulog. Men B 1H 9
Fron Pk. Av. L'chan 5B 12
Fron Rd. Old C 4C 22
Fron Uchaf. Col B 5J 21

G

Gadlas Rd. L'faen 6K 23
Gadlys La. Beau . . . . 2J 7 (off Castle St.)
Gaingc Rd. Tow 4D 26
Gallt y Sil. C'fon 5E 4
Gamar Rd. L'faen 5K 23
Gamlin St. Rhyl 6B 28
Gannock Pk. Deg 2F 19
Gannock Pk. W. Deg 2F 19
Gannock Rd. Deg 2F 19
Gaol St. Beau 1J 7
Garage St. L'no 4H 15
Gardd Denman. Ban 4C 10
Gardd Eryri. P'awr 5J 13
Garden Dri. Pen B 5E 16
Garden St. L'no 3G 15
Gareth Clo. Rhyl 7D 28
Garford Rd. Rhyl 4E 28
Garnett Av. Rhyl 7A 28
Garnett Dri. Pres 4H 29
Gth. Clarendon. Kin B 4J 27
Gth. Gopa. L'las 4B 24
Gth. Mill. Ban 1E 10
Gth. Morfa. Kin B 4J 27
Garth Rd. Old C 4B 22
Garth Rd. N. Moch 3F 21
Garth Rd. S. Moch 3F 21
Garthwen. L'chan 4B 12
Garwyn Av. Pres 6B 30
Gele Av. Aber 6K 25
Gelli For. Rhyl 7F 29
Gemig St. St As 6C 38
George St. L'no 3G 15
Gerddi. Glyn 6C 6
Gerddi Menai. C'fon 2D 4
Gerddi'r Morfa. Con 4E 18
Gerddi Stanley. Beau 1J 7
Ger-y-Glyn. D'chi 7K 13
Ger-y-Mor. Aber 3K 25
Ger y Mynydd. Ban 2E 10
Geufron. Rhyl 6C 28
Geulan Rd. L'faen 6H 23
Gilfach. Llan J 4K 19
Gilfach Goch. Men B 1J 9
Gilfach Rd. Llan J 2C 20

42 A-Z Bangor

Gilfach Rd. *P'awr* 3J 13
Gilfach Wen. *Men B* 1J 9
Gillian Clo. *Rhyl* 1E 32
Gillian Dri. *Rhyl* 2E 32
Gipsy La. *Kin B* 4A 32
Gladys Gro. *Col B* 3A 22
Glanaber Trad. Est. *Rhyl* 6D 28
Glanafon Ter. *Con* 7F 19
Glan Cadnant. *C'fon* 4E 4
Glandwr. *Pres* 3A 30
Glandwr Cres. *Kin B* 3H 27
Glan Ffyddion. *Dys* 2A 34
Glan Llyn. *L'yll* 3C 8
Glan Menai. *Tre* 6H 9
Glan Mor. *C'fon* 4C 4
Glan Mor. *Pres* 2C 30
Glan Morfa. *Tow* 4F 27
Glan Morfa Cvn. Pk. *Llan J* . . .5K 19
Glanmorfa Ind. Est. *Rhyl* 1A 32
Glan Mor. *L'chan* 4B 12
Glan Mor Ucha. *C'fon* 4C 4
Glan Peris. *C'fon* 4F 5
Glanrafon. *Aber* 6K 25
Glanrafon. *Ban* 2D 10
Glanrafon Av. *L'no* 3B 16
Glanrafon Ter. *St As* 6C 38
(off Lower St.)
Glan Rd. *Moch* 3F 21
Glan Seiont. *C'fon* 6E 4
Glan Traeth. *Ban* 2G 11
Glan Traeth. *Pres* 2C 30
Glanyfelin. *L'fan* 6B 6
(off Caerfelin)
Glan-y-Gors. *Pres* 3B 30
Glan-y-Mor. *Aber* 4J 25
Glan-y-Mor. *C'fon* 4C 4
Glan y Mor Pde. *L'no* 2G 15
Glan y Mor Pas. *L'no* 3G 15
(off Glan y Mor Pde.)
Glan-y-Mor Rd. *Deg & Llan J*
. . . . .3G 19
Glan-y-Mor Rd. *Pen B* 4D 16
Glan-y-Mor Rd. *Tan* 3F 23
Glan-yr-Afon Rd. *D'chi* 6J 13
Glan-yr-Afon Rd. *L'chan* 5E 12
Glan-y-Wern. *Moch & Bron* . . .2F 21
Glas Coed. *Col B* 5G 23
Glascoed. *Llan J* 3K 19
Glascoed Av. *Kin B* 2G 27
Glascoed Rd. *Aber* 7E 36
Glasfryn Av. *Pres* 6C 30
Glendower Ct. *Rhyl* 5C 28
(off Kinard Dri.)
Glenfor. *Aber* 6J 25
Gloddaeth Av. *L'no* 4E 14
Gloddaeth Cres. *L'no* 3H 15
Gloddaeth La. *L'no* 1J 19
(in two parts)
Gloddaeth St. *L'no* 3F 15
Gloddaeth Vw. *Pen B* 5C 16
Glyn Av. *Aber* 5J 25
Glyn Av. *Col B* 5B 22
Glyn Av. *Pres* 3D 30
Glyn Av. *Rhyl* 4F 33
Glyn Av. *Rhyl* 7E 28
Glyn Circ. *Kin B* 3J 27
Glyndwr Rd. *L'faen* 5K 23
Glyn Gth. Ct. *Men B* 6C 6
Glyn Gth. M. *Glyn* 6C 6
Glyn Isaf. *Llan J* 4K 19
Glyn Path. *D'chi* 7K 13
Glyn Ter. *P'awr* 7K 13
Glyn-y-Marl Gdns. *Llan J* 5K 19
Glyn-y-Marl Rd. *Llan J* 5K 19
Gogarth Av. *D'chi* 6H 13
Gogarth Rd. *L'no* 3E 14
Golden Gro. *Rhyl* 1D 32
Goleufryn. *Ban* 6K 9
Golygfa Sychnant. *D'chi* 6J 13
Gomer Ct. *Aber* 5J 25
(off Heol Gomer)
Gordon Av. *Pres* 5C 30
Gordon Av. *R Sea* 6H 17
Gordon Av. *Rhyl* 6A 28
Gorlan. *Con* 6E 18
Gorllewin Twthill. *C'fon* 4D 4
Goronwy Gdns. *Pen B* 5E 16
Gorphwysfa Av. *Pres* 2C 30
Gorsefield Rd. *Con* 4E 18
Gors Goch. *Men B* 1J 9
Gors Las. *Men B* 2J 9
Gors Rd. *Tow* 4F 27
(in three parts)
Gorwel. *L'chan* 5C 12
Gorwell. *Aber* 4K 25
Gower Rd. *Moch* 2F 21
Graham Av. *Pres* 6B 30

Graham Dri. *Rhyl* 5D 28
Graiglwyd Clo. *P'awr* 2K 13
Graiglwyd Rd. *P'awr* 3J 13
Graiglwyd Ter. *P'awr* 3J 13
Grange Av. *Rhyl* 6D 28
Grange Ct. *Rhyl* 6E 28
Grange Rd. *Ban* 4A 22
Grange Rd. *L'hos* 7H 15
Grange Rd. *Rhyl* 6C 28
Granville Ter. *P'awr* 2G 13
Grasmere Clo. *Pres* 2B 30
Grass Rd. *G'rdd M* 7E 36
Gt. Ormes Rd. *L'no* 3E 14
Green Av. *Kin B* 3K 27
Green Bank. *Ban* 7F 7
Green Cotts. *Beau* 1K 7
Green Edge. *Beau* 1K 7
Greenfield Rd. *Col B* 3A 22
Greenfield St. *Rhyl* 6C 28
Green Hill. *Old C* 4D 22
Grn. Lanes. *Pres* 3H 29
Green Rd. *R Sea* 7J 17
Greenway. *R Sea* 5H 17
Gregory Av. *Col B* 2H 21
Gregory Clo. *Col B* 2H 21
Gregory Cres. *Col B* 2H 21
Grenville Av. *Rhud* 5F 33
Grenville Row. *Bod* 3D 36
Groesffordd. *D'chi* 6H 13
(in two parts)
Groesffordd La. *P'awr* 2K 13
Groes Lwyd. *Aber* 5J 25
Groes Rd. *Col B* 4B 22
Gronant Hill. *Gron* 2J 31
Gronant Rd. *Pres* 3D 30
Gronant St. *Rhyl* 6A 28
Groome Av. *Rhyl* 1D 32
Grosvenor Av. *Rhyl* 7E 28
Grosvenor Rd. *Col B* 2J 21
Grosvenor Rd. *Pres* 2A 30
Grosvenor Rd. *Rhyl* 4D 28
Grove Pk. *Col B* 3A 22
Grove Pk. Av. *Rhyl* 5D 28
Grove Pk. W. *Col B* 3K 21
Grove Pas. *L'no* 2F 15
(off Tudno St.)
Grove Rd. *Col B* 3A 22
Grove, The. *Rhyl* 7C 30
Grove, The. *Rhyl* 5C 28
Gurnard Pl. *Rhyl* 2D 32
Gwalia Av. *Rhyl* 7C 28
Gwel Eryri. *L'fan* 5B 6
Gwel-Fryn. *Moch* 4F 21
Gwelfryn. *Pres* 3C 30
Gwellyn Av. *Kin B* 5J 27
Gwel yr Wyddfa. *Men B* 1J 9
Gwenarth Dri. *Rhyl* 2E 32
Gwern Las. *Ban* 4F 11
Gwindy St. *Rhud* 5E 32
Gwydyr Gdns. *L'no* 5J 15
Gwydyr Rd. *L'no* 5H 15
Gwyllt Rd. *L'chan* 7A 12
Gwynan Rd. *P'awr* 2J 13
Gwynant Rd. *L'no* 5H 15
Gwynedd Rd. *L'no* 3J 15
Gwynfryn Av. *Rhyl* 7B 28
Gwynfryn Ter. *L'faen* 5K 23
Gwynt y Mor. *Con* 3E 18
Gwytherin Av. *Tow* 3F 27

H

Hadden Ct. *R Sea* 6J 17
Haddon Clo. *Rhyl* 7B 28
Hadley Cres. *Rhyl* 5D 28
Hafan yr Ewyn. *Kin B* 4J 27
Hafan yr Heli. *Kin B* 4K 27
Hafod Av. *Kin B* 5K 27
Hafod Rd. *Pres* 2D 30
Hafod Rd. E. *Pen B* 4E 16
Hafod Rd. W. *Pen B* 4E 16
Hafodty La. *Col B* 5G 21
Hafod-y-Mor. *Aber* 4K 25
Hafod y Mor. *Pres* 2D 30
Hall Rd. *Pen B* 5D 16
Hammond Ct. *Rhyl* 1D 32
Hampton Rd. *C'fon* 4D 4
Handsworth Cres. *Rhyl* 6E 28
Hanover Ct. *L'no* 4J 15
Hanover Ct. *R Sea* 7G 17
Happy Valley Rd. *L'no* 1G 15
Harcourt Rd. *L'no* 4J 15
Harding Av. *Rhud* 6F 33
Hardwynn Dri. *Pres* 5B 30
Hardy Av. *Rhyl* 4D 28

Harlech Cres. *Pres* 4B 30
Harlech Rd. *L'no* 5H 15
Harp Ct. *Aber* 6K 25
Harrison Dri. *Kin B* 2H 27
Hartsville Av. *Pen B* 5D 16
Hawarden Rd. *Col B* 2K 21
Hawes Dri. *Deg* 1F 19
Hawthorn Av. *R Sea* 6H 17
Hayden Clo. *Col B* 5E 22
Haydn Clo. *Kin B* 2J 27
Hazel Ct. *Rhyl* 5E 28
Hazelwood Clo. *Col B* 3F 21
Heather Clo. *Old C* 4E 22
Heather Cres. *Pres* 5B 30
Heaton Pl. *R Sea* 1H 21
Heenan Rd. *Old C* 4E 22
Hen-Afon Rd. *Rhyl* 7E 28
Hendre Clo. *Rhud* 5F 33
Hendre Ct. *Pres* 4D 30
Hendre Rd. *Con* 7E 18
Hendwr La. *P'side* 4C 16
Hen Ffordd Conwy.
P'awr .2K 13
Henryd Rd. *Con* 7E 18
Henry's Av. *Bod* 3D 36
Henwalia. *C'fon* 5D 4
Heol Afon. *St As* 6B 38
Heol Aled. *Aber* 4H 25
Heol Awel. *Aber* 4H 25
Heol Belmont. *Ban* 3B 10
Heol Bodran. *Aber* 4H 25
Heol Clwyd. *St As* 6B 38
Heol Colwyn. *Aber* 4J 25
Heol Conwy. *Aber* 4H 25
Heol Dewi. *Aber* 6A 26
Heol Dewi. *Ban* 4C 10
Heol Dirion. *Col B* 5B 22
Heol Edward. *C'fon* 4D 4
Heol Elinor. *C'fon* 4D 4
Heol Elwy. *Aber* 4H 25
Heol Esgob. *St As* 6K 37
Heol Fryn. *Moch* 4F 21
Heol Gelert. *C'fon* 5D 4
Heol Gomer. *Aber* 5J 25
Heol Heddwch. *Aber* 5J 25
Heol Hendre. *Rhud* 5F 33
Heol Hir. *Aber* 5J 25
Heol Victoria. *Ban* 2C 10
Heol y Bryn. *C'fon* 4D 4
Heol-y-Coed. *Aber* 4J 25
Heol y Fedwen. *Aber* 5B 26
Heol-y-Llys. *Rhyl* 6F 29
Herkomer Cres. *L'no* 5E 14
Herkomer Rd. *L'no* 5E 14
Heron Way. *Deg* 2F 19
Hesketh Rd. *Old C* 4C 22
Heulfryn. *Deg* 3H 19
Hewitt Clo. *Pen B* 5C 16
Highbury Av. *Pres* 2C 30
Highbury Clo. *Pres* 1D 30
Highbury Cres. *Pres* 2C 30
Highfield Pk. *Aber* 6K 25
Highfield Pk. *Rhyl* 5C 28
Highfield Rd. *Col B* 4A 22
Highlands Clo. *Rhud* 4F 33
Highlands Rd. *Old C* 4G 23
Highland's Rd. *Rhud* 4E 32
High La. *R Sea* 7H 17
High St. *Aber* 6K 25
High St. *Con* 5G 19
High St. *Dys* 3B 34
High St. *Pres* 3D 30
High St. *Rhud* 5E 32
High St. *Rhyl* 5B 28
High St. *St As* 6C 38
High St. *Trel* 2J 35
Hillcrest Ct. *Bod* 5E 36
Hillcrest Rd. *Deg* 3H 19
Hillside. *St As* 6C 38
Hillside Av. *Old C* 4C 22
Hillside Rd. *Col B* 3K 21
Hillside Ter. *L'no* 2F 15
Hill Ter. *L'no* 2G 15
Hilltop Rd. *Rhyl* 1E 32
Hill Vw. Clo. *L'hos* 7J 15
Hill Vw. Ct. *L'hos* 7H 15
Hill Vw. Rd. *L'hos* 7H 15
Hilton Dri. *Rhyl* 4E 28
Hiraddug Pk. *Dys* 3B 34
Hiraddug Rd. *Dys* 3C 34
Holbeck Rd. *R Sea* 4J 17
Holland Dri. *Aber* 5B 26
Holland Pk. Dri. *Rhyl* 1E 32
Holly Clo. *Rhyl* 5E 28
Holyrood Av. *Old C* 4C 22
Holyrood Ct. *L'no* 5E 14
Holywell Cres. *Kin B* 4J 27

Holywell Rd. *St As* 5E 38
Honeysuckle La. *Col B* 5J 21
(in two parts)
Hope St. *Rhyl* 6A 28
Horton Dri. *R Sea* 1G 21
Hospital Rd. *L'no* 5G 15
Howard Pl. *L'no* 4G 15
Howard Rd. *L'no* 4G 15
Howell Av. *Rhud* 4F 33
Howell Dri. *Rhyl* 7F 29
Hyfrydle. *C'fon* 5E 4
Hyfrydle. *Dys* 3A 34
Hylas La. *Rhud* 6F 33
Hywel Pl. *L'no* 4G 15

I

Invalids' Wlk. *L'no* 3E 14
Iola Dri. *Old C* 4E 22
Irene Av. *Pres* 4J 29
Irving Rd. *L'no* 3J 15
Isallt Rd. *L'faen* 7J 23
Iscoed. *Beau* 1H 7
Isfryn. *Col B* 5G 23
Isfryn Rd. *Pres* 2C 30
(in two parts)
Isgoed. *Con* 7F 19
Isis Ct. *L'no* 5J 15
Islwyn Av. *Rhyl* 5D 28
Is Terfyn. *St As* 6B 38
Ivy St. *Col B* 3A 22

J

Jackson's Ct. *L'no* 4H 15
Jaclyn Clo. *Pres* 3J 29
James's Pk. *Dys* 3B 34
James St. *Ban* 2E 10
James St. *L'no* 3F 15
John's Dri. *Bod* 3D 36
John St. *L'no* 3G 15
John St. *Rhyl* 6A 28
Jubilee Pas. *L'no* 4G 15
(off Jubilee St.)
Jubilee St. *L'no* 4G 15
Juniper Way. *Rhyl* 5E 28

K

Kearsley Dri. *Rhyl* 1F 33
Keens Rd. *St As* 6B 38
Kendal Dri. *Kin B* 2H 27
Kenelm Rd. *R Sea* 7J 17
Kenneth Av. *Col B* 4A 22
Kensington Av. *Old C* 3C 22
Kentigern Ct. *St As* 6C 38
Kerfoot Av. *Rhud* 5E 32
Kimberley Rd. *Llan J* 5K 19
Kinard Dri. *Rhyl* 5C 28
King's Av. *L'no* 4F 15
Kings Av. *Pres* 3D 30
Kings Av. *Rhyl* 6B 28
Kings Dri. *Col B* 3J 21
King's Dri. *L'no* 4F 15
(off King's Rd.)
Kingsley Av. *Rhyl* 7C 28
Kings Oak. *Col B* 3H 21
King's Pl. *L'no* 4F 15
Kings Rd. *Col B* 3J 21
King's Rd. *L'no* 5F 15
King's Rd. *Old C* 4E 22
Kingston Rd. *Rhyl* 6A 28
Kingsway. *Aber* 3K 25
Kingsway. *Col B* 2K 21
Kingsway. *Kin B* 5J 27
Kingsway. *L'no* 4J 15
Kingsway. *Pres* 3E 30
Kingswood Pl. *Aber* 5H 25
Kinmel Av. *Aber* 4J 25
Kinmel Clo. *Kin B* 2H 27
Kinmel Dri. *Kin B* 2G 27
(Dinas Av.)
Kinmel Dri. *Kin B* 4D 36
(Engine Hill)
Kinmel Pk. Ind. Est.
Bod 4E 36
Kinmel St. *Rhyl* 6B 28
Kinmel Ter. *Rhyl* 6B 28
Kinmel Way. *Tow* 4F 27
Kirby Av. *Pres* 2F 31
Knowles Av. *Pres* 4C 30
Knowles Av. *Rhyl* 4E 28
Knowles Rd. *L'no* 4F 15
Knowsley Av. *Rhyl* 6D 28

Kyffin Clo. Old C 4C 22
Kynaston Rd. Pres 3J 29

L

Laburnum Dri. Rhyl 6E 28
Lake Av. Rhyl 7A 28
Lancaster Sq. Con 5G 19
Landsdowne Rd. Col B 2J 21
Langford Dri. Kin B 2G 27
Langley Clo. Pen B 5E 16
Larch Dri. Rhyl 5E 28
Larkmount Rd. Rhyl 6E 28
Laurel Ct. Rhyl 5E 28
Laurel Gro. M. Tow 4F 27
Lawn, The. Rhyl 5C 28
Lawson Rd. Col B 3A 22
Lees Rd. L'no 4F 15
Leonard Av. Rhyl 7E 28
Leslie Ter. St As 6C 38
(off Lower St.)
Lewis Clo. L'no 5J 15
Lichfield Dri. Pres 3A 30
Liddel Dri. L'no 5J 15
Lilac Av. Rhyl 6E 28
Linden Clo. Pres 3E 30
Linden Dri. Pres 4E 30
Linden Wlk. Pres 3E 30
Links Av. R Sea 5G 17
Links Av. Rhud 5F 33
Links, The. Pen B 6E 16
Little La. Beau 1K 7
Llain yr Eglwys. Ban 2E 10
Llain yr Ysgol. Maes 4C 10
Llain yr Ysgol. Maes 3F 11
Llanasa Rd. Gron 2J 31
(in two parts)
Llanberch-y-Mor. P'awr 2J 13
Llandaff Dri. Pres 3A 30
Llanddulas Av. Kin B 4J 27
Llanddulas Rd. Aber 4F 25
Llandudno Rd. Pen B 5D 16
Llandygai Ind. Est. L'gai 4G 11
Llanelian Heights. Old C 6D 22
Llanelian Rd. Old C 4C 22
Llanerch Rd. L'chan 7B 12
Llanfair Rd. Aber 7J 25
Llannerch Rd. E. R Sea 1J 21
Llannerch Rd. W. R Sea 1H 21
Llanrhos Rd. Pen B 6D 16
Llanrwst Rd. Col B 2H 21
Llanrwst Rd. Con 7F 19
Llawr Pentre. Old C 4D 22
Llewelyn Av. L'no 2F 15
Llewelyn Ct. Rhyl 7F 29
Llewelyn Rd. Col B 3K 21
Llewelyn St. Con 5G 19
Llewelyn Vw. R Sea 1F 21
Llican Ter. L'no 2E 14
(off Ty-Gwyn Rd.)
Llindir Rd. L'las 5A 24
Lloyd George Clo. L'no 5G 15
Lloyd Pas. L'no 3F 15
Lloyd St. L'no 3F 15
Lloyd St. W. L'no 4E 14
Llugwy Rd. Kin B 3H 27
Llwybr Cwfaint. Ban 3C 10
Llwybr Jinwbili. D'chi 7H 13
Llwyd Gro. Col B 4B 22
Llwyn Ceirios. C'fon 3E 4
Llwyn Elwy. St As 7B 38
Llwyn Estyn. Deg 3J 19
Llwyn Gwgan. L'chan 6B 12
Llwyn Harlech. Bod 3E 36
Llwyn Hudol. Ban 2F 11
Llwyn Isaf. Con 6F 19
Llwyn Morfa. Aber 5K 25
Llwynon Gdns. L'no 2F 15
Llwyn Onn. Aber 6J 25
Llwyn Onn. Gwae 6F 31
Llwyn Onn. R Sea 6H 17
Llwyn Onn. St As 7C 38
Llwynon Rd. L'no 2E 14
Llwyn Rhuthun. Bod 3E 36
Llwyn Uchaf. Aber 6J 25
Llwyn y Gog. L'chan 6B 12
Llys Aderyn Du. Rhyl 5G 29
Llys Alarch. Rhyl 6F 29
Llys Alun. St As 7C 38
Llys Alwen. Rhyl 6F 29
Llys Argoed. Col B 4J 21
Llys Arthur. Tow 4F 27
Llys Barham. C'fon 2E 4
Llys Bedwen. Rhyl 5F 29
Llys Bedwyr. Ban 2F 11
Llys Berllan. Gron 2J 31

Llys Bodlondeb. Con 5F 19
Llys Bodnant. Rhyl 6F 29
Llys Branwen. Rhyl 3H 27
Llys Brenig. Rhyl 6F 29
Llys Brierley. L'no 5J 15
Llys Cadnant. Rhyl 6F 29
Llys Cadwaladr. Maes 3F 11
Llys Caradoc. Tow 4F 27
Llys Catrin. Rhyl 5F 29
Llys Celyn. Pres 7B 30
Llys Charles. Tow 4F 27
Llys Clwyd. Kin B 1J 27
Llys Clwyd. P'awr 2J 13
Llys Clwyd. St As 7C 38
Llys Colomen. Rhyl 6G 29
Llys Colwyn. Old C 5D 22
Llys Cowlyd. Rhyl 6F 29
Llys Cregyn. Kin B 2J 27
Llys Cynan. Kin B 1J 27
Llys Dedwydd. R Sea 1H 21
Llys Dedwydd. Rhyl 5F 29
Llys Delyn. Rhyl 6F 29
Llys Dewi. Gron 2J 31
Llys Dewi. Rhyl 5F 29
Llys Dewi Sant. Ban 4C 10
Llys Dinas. Rhyl 6F 29
Llys Dyffryn. St As 7D 38
Llys Dyfrig. Ban 2G 11
Llys Ednyfed. Moch 3F 21
Llys Edward. Gron 2K 31
Llys Edward. Tow 4F 27
Llys Eirlys. Rhyl 5F 29
Llys Emrys. Ban 1F 11
Llys Eos. Rhyl 5G 29
Llysfaen Av. Kin B 2H 27
Llysfaen Rd. Col B 4E 22
Llysfaen Sta. Rd. L'faen 4J 23
Llys Gele. Aber 5K 25
Llys Geraint. Ban 2G 11
Llys Glan Aber. Rhyl 7C 28
Llys Glanrafon Kin B 2J 27
Llys Glyndwr. Tow 4F 27
Llys Gwylan. L'no 5H 15
(off Lon Cymru)
Llys Gwylan. Rhyl 6F 29
Llys Gwyn. C'fon 3E 4
Llys Gwyn. Pen B 4E 16
Llys Gwynant. Rhyl 6F 29
Llys Helig Dri. L'no 1B 14
Llys Helyg. Deg 1F 19
Llys Helyg. Rhyl 5F 29
Llys Hendre. Rhud 5F 33
Llys Idris. St As 6C 38
Llys Iwan. Gron 2J 31
Llys Llewelyn. Tow 4F 27
Llys Mabon. Ban 2F 11
Llys Madoc. Tow 4F 27
Llys Maelgwn. L'no 3F 15
Llys Mair. Ban 4B 10
Llys Marni. Aber 5K 25
Llys Meirion. C'fon 2E 4
Llys Miaren. Rhyl 5F 29
Llys Morgan. Rhyl 7D 28
Llys Mostyn. Trel 2J 35
Llys Offa. Trel 2J 35
Llys Owain. Ban 2F 11
Llys Owen. Gron 2J 31
Llys Padarn. Rhyl 6F 29
Llys Parc. R Sea 6H 17
Llys Pendefig. Kin B 2H 27
Llys Pentre Isaf. Col B 6E 22
Llys Pen y Ffordd. Rhud 4F 33
Llys Peris. Rhyl 6F 29
Llys Robin Goch. Rhyl 6F 29
Llys Sambrook. P'awr 1J 13
Llys Seiriol. L'no 4F 15
Llys Siabod. C'fon 5E 4
Llys Sion. Rhyl 5F 29
Llys Sychnant. Con 7E 18
Llys Tegid. Rhyl 6F 29
Llys Trewithan. St As 5C 38
Llys Tryfan. C'fon 5E 4
Llys Tudor. Tow 4F 27
Llys Tudur. Rhyl 5F 29
Llys y Foel. C'fon 5E 4
Llys y Foel Bungalows. C'fon 5D 4
(off Ffordd Eryri)
Llys y Garn. C'fon 6D 4
Llys-y-Gerddi. Rhyl 1D 32
Llys-y-Goppa. Aber 7H 25
Llys-y-Marchog. Kin B 2H 27
Llys-y-Mor. Aber 4J 25
Llys yr Eifl. C'fon 6D 4
Llys-yr-Eos. Aber 5B 26
Llys-y-Wyddfa. Rhyl 5F 29
Llys-y-Tywysog. Rhyl 5F 29

Lon Aeron. Rhyl 5F 29
Lon Alwen. Pres 3D 30
Lon Arfon. C'fon 5E 4
Lon Bach. C'fon 4E 4
Lon Bedw. Rhyl 5F 29
Lon Brynli. Pres 4A 30
Lon Bryn Teg. L'fan 6C 6
Lon Bulkeley. Men B 1H 9
Lon Cadfan. Pres 5A 30
Lon Cae Darbi. C'fon 4G 5
Lon Cae Ffynnon. C'fon 4G 5
Lon Cae Sel. C'fon 4D 4
Lon Cambell. C'fon 2D 4
Lon Caradog. Aber 6H 25
Lon Cariadon. Ban 2E 10
Lon Cariadon. Men B 3K 9
Lon Cefn Du. C'fon 5E 4
Lon Cei Bont. Men B 3K 9
Lon Ceiriog. Pres 5A 30
Lon Ceirios. Aber 7H 25
Lon Celynnen. Rhyl 6F 29
Lon Cilgwyn. C'fon 6E 4
Lon Coed Helen. C'fon 5C 4
Lon Crwyn. C'fon 4C 4
(off Lon y Felin)
Lon Cwybr. Rhud 4E 32
Lon Cymru. L'no 5H 15
Lon Cynan. Aber 6H 25
Lon Cynan. Pres 4A 30
Lon Cytir. Ban 7K 9
Lon Dawel. Aber 7J 25
Lon Dderwen. Aber 7H 25
Lon Ddewi. C'fon 3D 4
Lon Dwdr. Tal 5J 11
Lon Deg. Aber 7J 25
Lon Delyn. Pres 2D 30
Lon Derw. Rhyl 7J 25
Lon Dinorben. Aber 6J 25
London Rd. Trel 2G 35
Lon Drych. L'yll 3E 8
Lon Dyfi. Pres 3K 29
Lon Eglyn. Rhyl 5F 29
Lon Eilian. C'fon 5E 4
Lon Eirin. Tow 5F 27
Lon Eirlys. Pres 2D 30
Lon Elan. Pres 6B 30
Lon Eryri. Ban 4B 10
Lon Evelyn. Ban 2D 10
Lon Fach. L'no 4G 15
(off Norman Rd.)
Lon Ffawydd. Aber 6J 25
Lon Foel Graig. L'yll 3E 8
(in two parts)
Lon Frondeg. Ban 2E 10
Lon Gadlas. Aber 6J 25
Lon Ganol. Men B 2H 9
Lon Garnedd. Aber 6J 25
Lon Garth. Men B 2H 9
Lon Gernant. Men B 2J 9
Lon Glanfor. Aber 5A 26
Lon Glan Mor. Ban 1F 11
Longleat Av. L'no 3B 16
Lon Glyd. Aber 5B 26
Lon Glyndwr. Aber 6H 25
Lon Goed. Aber 7J 25
Lon Goed. Llan J 4J 19
Lon Graig. L'yll 3E 8
Lon Gwalia. L'no 5J 15
Lon Gwyndaf. Pres 4A 30
Lon Hafan. Aber 7J 25
Lon Hedydd. L'yll 3E 8
Lon Hedyn. Rhyl 5F 29
Lon Helen. C'fon 5E 4
Lon Helyg. Aber 7H 25
Lon Hen Felin. C'fon 4G 5
Lon Heulog. Aber 7J 25
Lon Heulog. Kin B 4H 27
Lon Hyfryd. Aber 7J 25
Lon Isaf. Men B 1J 9
Lon Islwyn. Pres 5A 30
Lon Kinmel. Aber 3K 25
Lon Las. Mon B 2K 9
Lon Lelog. Rhyl 5F 29
Lon Llewelyn. Aber 6H 25
Lon Mafon. Rhyl 5F 29
Lon Meirion. Ban 1E 10
Lon Melin Esgob. Ban 3E 10
Lon Menai. Men B 1H 9
Lon Mieri. Ban 4B 10
Lon Mynach. Pen B 4D 16
Lon Nant. C'fon 4E 4
Lon Ogwen. Aber 4B 10
Lon Oleuwen. C'fon 6E 4
Lon Olwen. Kin B 3H 27
Lon Padog. Con 4E 18
Lon Pant. L'yll 5D 4
Lon Parc. C'fon 5D 4

Lon Pendyffryn. L'las 4A 24
Lon Pen Nebo. Men B 2J 9
Lon Penrallt. Ban 2D 10
Lon Penrhiw. L'las 4A 24
Lon Pobty. Ban 4E 10
Lon Powys. Ban 4B 10
Lon Priestley. C'fon 3E 4
Lon Pwllfanogl. L'yll 4D 8
Lon Refail. L'yll 2E 8
Lon Rhosyn. Rhyl 5F 29
Lon Seiriol. Ban 1E 10
Lon Sydney. C'fon 3D 4
Lon Tabernacl. Ban 2E 10
Lon Taliesin. Pres 4A 30
Lon Temple. Ban 2D 10
Lon Tilsli. Pres 5A 30
Lon Totton. Ban 1E 10
Lon ty Bach. L'chan 7A 12
Lon ty Croes. L'yll 3D 8
Lon Tyddyn. Ban 3F 11
Lon ty Gwyn. C'fon 5E 4
Lon ty Mawr. L'fan 6B 6
Lon ty Newydd. C'fon 4G 5
Lon Ty'n y Caeau. Men B 2H 9
Lon Vardre. Deg 2G 19
Lon Warfield. C'fon 3D 4
Lon Wen. Aber 7J 25
Lon Wen. Rhyl 5F 29
Lon-y-Bedw. Aber 5B 10
Lon-y-Berllan. Aber 7J 25
Lon y Brodyr. Ban 1E 10
Lon-y-Bryn. Ban 4A 10
Lon y Bryn. C'fon 5E 4
Lon y Bryn. Men B 1H 9
Lon-y-Cyll. Aber 4K 25
Lon-y-Dail. Aber 7J 25
Lon-y-Der. Ban 4A 10
Lon-y-Dryw. Aber 5A 26
Lon y Dwr. Ban 1F 11
Lon-y-Felin. Ban 3F 11
Lon y Felin. C'fon 4C 4
Lon y Ffrith. L'no 4J 15
Lon-y-Ffrwd. Ban 4B 10
Lon-y-Gaer. Deg 3H 19
Lon y Gamfa. Men B 1J 9
Lon-y-Glyder. Ban 4B 10
Lon y Gogarth. Ban 1E 10
Lon-y-Gors. Aber 4K 25
Lon-y-Llyn. Aber 6A 26
Lon-y-Meillion. Ban 4B 10
Lon-y-Mes. Aber 7H 25
Lon y Parc. Ban 3G 11
Lon yr Efail. Glan 7C 16
Lon yr Eglwys. C'fon 4C 4
Lon Ysgol Rad. C'fon 4D 4
Lon Ysgubor Wen. C'fon 3E 4
Lon y Waen. Men B 1J 9
Lon-y-Waun. Aber 6J 25
Lon y Wennol. L'yll 2E 8
Lon y Wylan. Aber 5B 26
Lon y Wylan. L'yll 2E 8
Lorina Gro. L'no 5J 15
Lothian Pk. St As 6C 38
(off Bryn Gobaith)
Lwr. Denbigh Rd. St As 6B 38
Lwr. Foel Rd. Dys 4C 34
Lwr. Gate St. Con 5G 19
Lower St. Ban 3E 10
Lower St. St As 6C 38
Lowther Clo. Kin B 4J 27
Lowther Ct. Bod 3F 37
Luke St. St As 6C 38
Lynton Wlk. Rhyl 5D 28
Lynwood Dri. Rhyl 5D 28

M

McInroy Clo. L'no 5G 15
McKinley Rd. Llan J 5K 19
Madoc Clo. R Sea 7F 17
Madoc St. L'no 3G 15
Madryn Av. Rhyl 7D 28
Maelgwyn Dri. Deg 3H 19
Maelgwyn Rd. L'no 3F 15
Maenafon. L'yll 3D 8
Maenan. Col B 5G 23
Maen Gwyn. Aber 6H 25
Maes Alaw. Rhud 5E 32
Maes Alltwen. D'chi 6J 13
Maes Arthur. Rhyl 7F 29
Maes Awel. L'fan 7A 6
Maes Bedwen. Rhud 4E 32
Maes Benarth. Con 7G 19
Maes Berllan. L'no 5J 15
Maes Berllan. P'awr 2J 13

Maes Briallen. L'no 7G 15
Maes Bryn Melyd. Rhyl 7F 29
Maes Cadnant. C'fon 4E 4
Maes Canol. Aber 4K 25
Maes Canol. Llan J 4A 20
Maes Cefndy. Rhyl 7D 28
Maes Clwyd. Rhyl 7F 29
Maes Clyd. L'no 4J 15
Maes Cwm. Rhyl 7F 29
Maes Cwstennin. Llan J 5A 20
Maes Cybi. Aber 4K 25
Maes Cynbryd. L'las 4B 24
(in two parts)
Maes Derw. Llan J 5K 19
Maes Derwen. Rhud 5E 32
Maes Dolfor. L'chan 4B 12
Maesdu Av. L'no 5F 15
Maesdu Pl. L'no 5G 15
Maesdu Rd. L'no 5G 15
Maes Emlyn. Rhyl 5C 28
Maes Esgob. Dys 3A 34
Maes Famau. Rhyl 7F 29
Maes Ffyddion. Rhud 5E 32
Maes Ffynnon. L'las 4B 24
Maes Ffynnon. L'fan 4C 6
Maes Gaer. Rhyl 7F 29
Maes Gele. Aber 5B 26
Maes Glas. Dys 3A 34
Maes Glas. Llan J 3J 19
Maes Glas. Pres 2D 30
Maes Glas. R Sea 6H 17
Maes Gweryl. Con 6F 19
Maesgwynedd. C'fon 3E 4
Maesgwyn Rd. Pen B 5E 16
Maes Hafoty. L'wrn 1A 6
Maes Hedydd. Rhyl 6E 28
Maes Helyg. Rhud 5E 32
Maes Heulog. C'fon 3E 4
Maes Hiraddug. Dys 3C 34
Maeshyfryd. Ban 1E 10
Maes Hyfryd. Beau 1H 7
Maes Hyfryd. C'fon 3E 4
Maeshyfryd. Dys 3B 34
Maes Hyfryd. L'yll 3D 8
Maesincla. C'fon 3E 4
Maesincla La. C'fon 3E 4
Maes Isaf. Rhyl 7F 29
Maes Isalaw. Ban 1F 11
Maes Llewelyn. Rhyl 7E 28
Maes Madog. Llane 6D 22
Maes Maenefa. Rhyl 7G 29
Maes Mawr. Ban 5K 9
Maes Menlli. Rhyl 1F 33
Maes Meurig. Pres 6B 30
Maes Offa. Trel 2J 35
Maes Onnen. Rhud 4E 32
Maes Owen. Bod 3D 36
Maes Rhosyn. Rhud 4E 32
Maes Rhosyn. Tow 5E 26
Maes Seiriol. Aber 6A 26
Maes Stanley. Bod 3D 36
Maes Tegid. Pres 4C 30
Maes Tudno. Aber 6A 26
Maes Tyddyn To. Men B 2J 9
Maes-y-Bryn. Rhud 4F 33
Maes-y-Castell. L'hos 1G 19
Maes y Coed. Deg 2J 19
Maes y Coed. Men B 2K 9
Maes-y-Coed Av. Old C 4C 22
Maes-y-Cwm. L'no 5C 30
Maes-y-Don Dri. Rhyl 4D 28
Maes-y-Dre. Aber 6K 25
Maes y Dre. Gron 2J 31
Maes-y-Dref. Ban 2E 10
Maes-y-Foel. Dys 3B 34
Maes-y-Fron. Col B 5B 22
Maes-y-Fron. L'faen 5K 23
Maes-y-Glyn. Col B 5B 22
Maes-y-Glyn. L'chan 4B 12
Maes y Gog. Rhyl 5G 29
Maes-y-Groes. Pres 3C 30
(in two parts)
Maes y Gwenith. Pen B 5D 16
Maes y Llan. Con 7F 19
Maes y Llan. Tow 3E 26
Maes-y-Llan. D'chi 6H 13
Maes-y-Llys. Dys 3A 34
Maes-y-Mor. Aber 5B 26
(in two parts)
Maes y Mor. Pen B 4E 16
Maes y Parc. Rhyl 7F 29
Maes-yr-Hafod. Men B 1H 9
Maes yr Oredd. L'no 5G 15
Maes y Wennol. Pen B 5D 16
Maes y Wylan. Pen B 5D 16

Magnolia Ct. Rhyl 6E 28
Mall, The. Pres 1C 30
Malvern Ri. R Sea 6G 17
Manod Rd. Pres 6C 30
Manor Clo. Pres 4E 30
Manor Pk. L'no 3F 15
Manor Way. Kin B 2J 27
(in two parts)
Maple Av. Rhyl 6E 28
Marble Arch. L'no 3G 15
Marble Chu. Gro. Bod 3F 37
Marford Dri. Aber 6H 25
Margaret St. Beau 1J 7
Marian Pl. L'no 5F 15
Marian Rd. L'no 5F 15
Marie Clo. L'no 5D 16
Marine Av. Old C 4C 22
Marine Ct. Deg 1F 19
Marine Cres. Deg 2F 19
Marine Cres. P'awr 1J 13
Marine Dri. L'no . . . . . .1A 14 & 1G 15
Marine Dri. R Sea 5G 17
Marine Dri. Rhyl 4D 28
Marine Gdns. Deg 1F 19
Marine Path. Old C 4C 22
Marine Rd. Col B 2K 21
Marine Rd. Pen B 5E 16
Marine Rd. Pens 3K 25
Marine Rd. Pres 2C 30
Marine Rd. E. Pres 1E 30
Marine Ter. P'awr 1K 13
Marine Vw. R Sea 7F 17
Marine Wlk. Con 4F 19
Marion Rd. Pres 3K 29
Market Pl. Aber 5K 25
Market Dri. Rhyl 6B 28
Market St. Aber 5J 25
Marlborough Dri. R Sea 6G 17
Marlborough Gro. Rhyl 1K 27
Marlborough Pl. L'no 3H 15
(off Vaughan St.)
Marl Cres. Llan J 4J 19
Marl Dri. Llan J 3K 19
Marl Gdns. Deg 3J 19
Marl La. Deg & Llan J 2J 19
Marl Vw. Ter. Deg 3J 19
Marsh Rd. Rhud 5D 32
Marsh Rd. Rhyl 7A 28
Marston Dri. R Sea 7F 17
Marston Rd. R Sea 7F 17
Masonic St. L'no 2G 15
Maude St. Rhyl 6A 28
Mauldeth Rd. R Sea 7J 17
Mayfield Gro. Rhyl 5E 28
Meadowbank. Col B 6E 22
Meadow Gdns. L'no 5K 15
Meadows La. Pres 5C 30
Meadows, The. Pres 5B 30
Meadows Way. R Sea 7F 17
Meadway. R Sea 5H 17
Medea Dri. Rhyl 4D 28
Meiriadog Rd. Old C 4E 22
Meirion. Aber 3K 25
Meirion Clo. Rhyl 1D 32
Meirion Dri. Con 3E 18
Meirion Gdns. Col B 3A 22
Meliden Rd. Pres 6C 30
Meliden Rd. Rhud 4G 33
Melyd Av. Pres 5C 30
Menai Av. Rhyl 7B 28
Menai Vw. Ter. Ban 2C 10
Menai Ville Ter. Men B 2K 9
Mercia Dri. Rhyl 4D 28
Meredith Cres. Rhyl 7C 28
Merfyn Way. Rhyl 7F 29
Merivale Rd. Pen B 5E 16
Merllyn Rd. Rhyl 6E 28
Merllyn Ter. St As 6B 38
Merton Pk. P'awr 2K 13
Merton Pl. Rhyl 2E 32
Methven Dri. Pres 3J 29
Mews, The. Llan J 3J 19
Michaels Rd. Rhyl 1E 32
Mile Rd., The. L'fan & Beau 3E 6
Millbank Rd. Rhyl 6C 28
Mill Dri. Col B 4D 22
Mill Hill. Con 7F 19
Milla. Beau 1J 7
Mill Rd. L'chan 5B 12
Mill St. L'las 4B 24
Mill St. St As 5C 38
Milmor Way. Pres 3A 30
Minafon. Ban 3D 10
Minafon. Old C 4D 22
Miners La. Old C 4F 23
Minffordd Rd. L'las 4A 24

Min Menai. Ban 4B 10
Min Ogwen. T'bont 6J 11
Min-y-Coed. Ban 3F 11
Min-y-Ddol. Ban 4F 11
Min-y-Don. Aber 4H 25
Min y Don. Pen B 3E 16
Min-y-Don Av. Old C 3C 22
Min-y-Don Dri. Old C 3D 22
Min-y-Don Rd. Old C 3D 22
Min-y-Ffrwd. L'yll 3D 8
Min y Morfa. Pres 3B 30
Min-y-Morfa. Tow 4F 27
Mochdre Bus. Pk. Moch 4E 20
Mochdre Rd. Col B 5F 21
Moel Eilio. C'fon 6E 4
Moel Vw. Rd. Gron 1J 31
Moelwyn Av. E. Kin B 2J 27
Moelwyn Av. N. Kin B 1H 27
Moelwyn Av. W. Kin B 2H 27
Molineaux Rd. Rhyl 4E 28
Mona Dri. D'chi 6H 13
Mona Rd. Con 4E 18
Mona Ter. L'chan 3D 12
Mona Ter. Rhyl 6C 28
Monks' Path. L'no 1C 14
Monmouth Gro. Pres 3A 30
Moon St. L'no 3H 15
Moor Pk. Aber 3K 25
Moranedd Ct. L'las 3A 24
Mor Awel. Aber 4J 25
Mor Awel. Col B 4G 23
Morfa Av. Kin B 3G 27
Morfa Bach. Rhyl 7C 28
Morfa Clo. Pres 4A 30
Morfa Conwy Bus. Pk.
Con 4C 18
Morfa Dri. Con 4C 18
Morfa Rd. L'no 4E 14
Morfa Rd. Pen B 5E 16
Morfa Vw. Bod 3E 36
Morgan Rd. Pres 3K 29
Morlais. Aber 5A 26
Morlais. Con 5A 18
Morlan Pk. Rhyl 5B 28
Morley Rd. L'no 4J 15
Morley Rd. Rhyl 6C 28
Mornant Av. Pres 1D 30
Morris Av. Pres 3K 29
Morris Clo. Pen B 5D 16
Moss Dri. Rhyl 4J 15
Mossley Mt. Pen B 5D 16
Mostyn Av. L'no 4J 15
Mostyn Av. Pres 3E 30
Mostyn Broadway. L'no 3H 15
Mostyn Champneys Retail Pk.
L'no 4J 15
Mostyn Cres. L'no 3H 15
Mostyn Rd. Col B 2K 21
Mostyn Rd. Gron 2H 31
Mostyn St. L'no 2G 15
Mountain La. P'awr 2K 13
Mountain Rd. Con 5E 18
Mt. Ida Rd. Pres 4E 30
Mount Park. Con 6F 19
Mount Pleasant. Beau 1J 7
(off Rating Row)
Mount Pleasant. Con 6F 19
Mt. Pleasant Sq. C'fon 4D 4
(off Pentre Newydd)
Mt. Pleasant Ter. P'side 4C 16
Mount Rd. L'chan 5C 12
Mount Rd. St As 4B 38
Mowbray Rd. L'no 4J 15
Mulberry Clo. Con 3E 18
Mynydd La. Col B 5F 21

Nant Clo. Rhud 4F 33
Nant Dri. Pres 2E 30
Nant Hall Rd. Pres 3D 30
Nant Ter. Men B 2K 9
Nant-y-Berllan. L'chan 6C 12
Nant-y-Coed. Llan J 4A 20
Nant y Crai La. Gron 3H 31
Nantyfelin Rd. L'chan 6C 12
Nant-y-Gamar Rd. L'no 3K 15
Nant-y-Glyn. Llan J 4K 19
(in two parts)
Nant-y-Glyn Rd. Col B 7H 21
Nant y Gro. Gron 2J 31
Narrow La. Llan J 3A 20
Netley Rd. Rhyl 7B 28
Neuadd Alun. Ban 2D 10
(off Ffordd y Coleg)

Neuadd Arfon. Ban 3A 10
(off Ffordd Caergybi)
Neuadd Barlow/Barlows. Ban . . .3D 10
(off Lon Pobty)
Neuadd Cefn y Coed. Ban 2C 10
(off Heol Ffriddoedd)
Neuadd Dyfrdwy. Ban 2D 10
(off Ffordd y Coleg)
Neuadd Elidir. Ban 2C 10
(off Heol Ffriddoedd)
Neuadd Emrys Evans. Ban 2C 10
(off Rhodfa Menai)
Neuadd Eryri. Ban 2D 10
(off Ffordd y Coleg)
Neuadd John Morris Jones. Ban
. . . . .2E 10
(off Ffordd y Coleg)
Neuadd Llys Tryfan. Ban 3C 10
(off Heol Ffriddoedd)
Neuadd Mon. Ban 1D 10
(off Ffordd y Coleg)
Neuadd Plas Gwyn. Ban 2C 10
(off Rhodfa Menai)
Neuadd Rathbone. Ban 2C 10
(off Ffordd Garth Uchaf)
Neuadd Reichel. Ban 3B 10
(off Heol Ffriddoedd)
Neuadd Seiriol. Ban 3A 10
(off Ffordd Caergybi)
Neuadd y Borth. Ban 3C 10
(off Ffordd y Coleg)
Neuadd Y Glyder. Ban 3C 10
(off Heol Ffriddoedd)
Nevill Ct. L'no 3H 15
New Rd. L'las 5B 24
New Rd. Rhud 5F 33
Newry Dri. L'chan 6D 12
New St. Aber 6K 25
New St. Beau 1J 7
New St. Con 7F 19
New St. L'no 3F 15
Newton Rd. R Sea 6H 17
Norbreck Dri. Rhyl 1F 33
Norcliffe Av. Col B 4E 22
Norfolk Av. Pres 3D 30
Norman Dri. Rhyl 6C 28
Norman Rd. L'no 4G 15
Norman Way. L'no 4G 15
North Av. Pres 3C 30
North Av. Rhyl 6A 28
North Dri. Rhyl 1E 32
North Pde. L'no 2G 15
N. Wales Holiday Camp.
Aber 4B 26
N. Wales Path. Old C & L'faen
. . . . .6F 23
N. Wales Path. Pens 5A 26
N. Western Gdns. L'no 3H 15
Norton Av. Pres 2C 30
Norton Rd. L'no 3H 15
Norton Rd. R Sea 1H 21
Norwood Pas. L'no 3G 15
Nursery Clo. Pres 3C 30

O

Oak Dri. Col B 2H 21
Oak Dri. Clo. Col B 2H 21
Oak Hill Dri. Pres 4D 30
Oak Hill La. Pres 4D 30
(in two parts)
Oakland Av. Rhyl 7A 28
Oak La. St As 5C 38
Oaklea. Kin B 4J 27
Oaklea Ct. Rhyl 7E 28
Oakville Av. Rhyl 5E 28
Oakwood Rd. Rhyl 5D 28
Ochr y Bryn. Pres 7C 30
Offa's Dyke Path. Gwae 6D 30
Off Hill St. Men B 2K 9
Ogwen Av. Kin B 2K 27
Ogwen Ter. L'faen 5K 23
Old Conway Rd. Moch 4E 20
Old Foryd Rd. Kin B 1J 27
Old Gate. Pres 3J 29
Oldgate Rd. Pres 3J 29
Old Golf Rd. Rhyl 4D 28
Old Highway. Col B 3F 21
Old Mill Rd. D'chi 6J 13
Old Rd. Con 5F 19
Old Rd. L'no 2F 15
Olinda St. Rhyl 5C 28
Oliver Jones Dri. Pen B 5C 16
Olivia Dri. Rhyl 4D 28
Orchard Gro. Rhyl 3F 21
Orchard, The. Men B 1K 9

Orme Av. R Sea 5H 17
Orme Rd. Moch 3E 20
Ormeside. P'side 5C 16
Orme Ter. Ban 3C 10
(off Stryd Belmont)
Orme Vw. Ban 3C 10
Orme Vw. Dri. Pres 5D 30
Ormonde Ter. L'no 2E 14
Orton Gro. Rhyl 7A 28
Osborne Gdns. Rhyl 7A 28
Osborne Ter. Ban 1F 11
Oswald Rd. Llan J 5K 19
Oswalds. Ban 2C 10
(off Heol Victoria)
Oval, The. L'no 3F 15
Overlea Av. Deg 3H 19
Overlea Cres. Con 3H 19
Overton Av. Pres 3A 30
Owain Glyndwr. Kin B 3J 27
Owain Gwynedd. Kin B 3J 27
Owen Clo. Rhyl 1D 32
Oxford Gro. Rhyl 6B 28
Oxford Rd. L'no 4G 15
Oxwich Dri. Moch 3F 21

P

Pabo La. Llan J 3B 20
Paddock, The. Pres 6C 30
Paddock, The. St As 6C 38
Palace Av. Rhyl 6A 28
Palmeira Gdns. Pres 4D 30
Pandy Av. Kin B 4A 32
Pandy La. Dys 3C 34
Pant Glas. St As 5A 38
Panton St. Ban 2E 10
Pant Teg. Deg 4J 19
Pant-yr-Afon. P'awr 2J 13
Parade, The. L'no 3G 15
Paradise Cres. P'awr 2J 13
(off Brynmor Ter.)
Paradise Rd. P'awr 2J 13
Paradise St. Rhyl 6B 28
Parc Aberconway. Pres 3F 31
Parc Benarth. Con 7F 19
Parc Bodnant. L'chan 5H 15
Parc Bron Deg. Dys 4B 34
Parc Bryn Awelon. Old C 4F 23
Parc Cambria. Col B 4F 23
Parc Edith. Rhud 5E 32
Parc Esmor. Rhyl 5D 28
Parc Ffordd Las. Rhyl 7C 28
Parc Ffynon. L'faen 5K 23
Parc Foel Lus. P'awr 2K 13
Parc Glan Aber. Aber 5J 25
Parc Gwelfor. Dys 2B 34
Parc Gwynedd. Pen B 4D 16
Parc Henblas. L'chan 5B 12
Parc Hyde. Kin B 4J 27
Parciau Clo. Old C 4D 22
Parc Isaf. L'chan 4B 12
Parc Menai. L'chan 4B 12
Parc Nant Rd. L'chan 6C 12
Parc Offa. Trel 2J 35
Parc Sychnant. Con 6E 18
Parc Twr. L'yll 3E 8
Parc Victoria. Ban 2C 10
Parc-y-Lleng. Rhud 5E 32
Park Av. Bod 3D 36
Park Av. Kin B 3J 27
Park Av. L'no 4K 15
Park Cres. L'chan 4B 12
(in two parts)
Park Dri. Deg 3H 19
Park Dri. Rhyl 6D 28
Pk. Dyffryn Ind. Est.
Pres 3C 30
Park Elen. Kin B 4J 27
Park Gro. Aber 4J 25
Park La. L'no 4K 15
Park Luned. Kin B 4J 27
Park M. Deg 3G 19
Park Rd. Col B 3A 22
Park Rd. Deg 3H 19
Park Rd. L'chan 5B 12
Park St. Ban 2D 10
Park Ter. Deg 3H 19
Parkway. R Sea 6H 17
Parliament St. Rhud 5D 28
Patagonia Av. Rhyl 6D 28
Patrick Av. Rhyl 1E 32
Peel St. Aber 5K 25
Pencae. L'faen 6B 6
Penchwintan Ter. Ban 4B 10
Pencoed Av. L'las 5B 24
Pencoed Rd. L'las 5B 24

Pen Deitsh. C'fon 4C 4
Pendorlan. Rhud 5E 32
(off Castle St.)
Pendorlan Av. Col B 3A 22
Pendorlan Rd. Pen B 5F 17
Pendre Av. Pres 3D 30
Pendre Av. Rhyl 7E 28
Pendre Rd. P'side 4C 16
Pen Dyffryn. Llan J 4A 20
Pendyffryn Gdns. Pres 3D 30
Pendyffryn Rd. Rhyl 7D 28
Pendyffryn Rd. N. Rhyl 6E 28
Pengarth. Con 6E 18
Pengelli Wyn. C'fon 2F 5
Peniel St. Deg 3G 19
Penisaf Av. Tow 4E 26
Penlan. Aber 4K 25
Penlan. L'no 1F 19
Pen Lan. Tow 4E 26
Penley Av. Pres 3A 30
Penllech. C'fon 4D 4
(in two parts)
Pen Llyn. Pens 3K 25
Penlon. Men B 1H 9
Penlon Gdns. Ban 2F 11
Penmaen Ct. R Sea 1G 21
Penmaen Cres. Con 4E 18
Penmaen Cres. Maisonettes. Con
. . . . .4E 18
Penmaenmawr Rd.
L'chan 5B 12
Penmaen Rd. Con 4D 18
Pen Morfa. C'fon 6E 4
Pennant Ct. L'no 5H 15
Pennant Cres. Ban 4C 10
Pennant Gro. Pres 1D 30
Pen Rallt. Men B 1J 9
Penrallt Isaf. Ban 2D 10
Penrallt Isaf. C'fon 4D 4
Penrallt Uchaf. C'fon 4D 4
Penrhiw. Aber 6J 25
Penrhos. Aber 4K 25
Penrhos Av. Llan J 5K 19
Penrhos Av. Old C 4F 23
Penrhos Dri. Ban 4B 10
Penrhos Dri. Pen B 5E 16
Penrhos Rd. Col B 1K 21
Penrhyn Av. R Sea 5G 17
Penrhyn Beach. Pen B 4D 16
Penrhyn Beach E. Pen B 3E 16
Penrhyn Beach W. Pen B 4D 16
Penrhyn Clo. Pen B 4D 16
Penrhyn Cres. L'no 4D 4
(off Parade, The)
Penrhyn Dri. R Sea 5G 17
Penrhyn Hill. P'side 4C 16
Penrhyn-Isaf Rd. Pen B 5E 16
Penrhyn Madoc. L'no 6D 16
Penrhyn Old Rd. P'side & Pen B
. . . . .5C 16
(in two parts)
Penrhyn Pk. Pen B 5E 16
Penrhyn Pk. R Sea 6H 17
Penrhyn Rd. Col B 2K 21
Pensarn Ind. Est. Aber 3J 25
Pentir Av. Ban 4E 16
Pentraeth. Col B 4G 23
Pentre Av. Aber 5K 25
Pentregwyddel Rd.
L'faen 5J 23
Pentregwyddel Ter.
L'faen 5K 23
Pentre Isaf. Old C 6E 22
Pentre La. Gron 3K 31
Pentre La. Rhud 4F 33
Pentre Mawr. Aber 4K 25
Pentre Newydd. C'fon 4D 4
Pentre Newydd. Old C 5D 22
Pentre Ucha. Aber 5K 25
Pentre Uchaf. L'chan 6B 12
Pen Tywyn. Pres 3B 30
Pen-y-Berth. L'yll 3F 9
Pen-y-Bont Rd. L'nin 7D 16
Pen-y-Bryn. C'fon 7D 4
Penybryn. L'chan 6B 12
Pen-y-Bryn. Old C 4D 22
Pen-y-Bryn Rd. Col B 4H 21
Penybryn Rd. L'chan 5B 12
Pen-y-Cefndy. Rhyl 1D 32
Pen y Cwm. L'no 5G 15
Pen-y-Ffordd Ter. P'side 4C 16
Pen-y-Gaer. Deg 3H 19
Pen y Garreg La. Pen B 4D 16
Pen-y-Garth. C'fon 3D 4
Pen-y-Llys. Rhyl 6F 29
Pen-y-Maes. Aber 4K 25

Pen-y-Maes. Pres 7C 30
Pen-y-Maes Av. Rhyl 7F 29
Pen-y-Mynydd. Col B 4H 21
Pen-y-Parc. P'side 4C 16
Pen-y-Wern. Ban 5B 10
Pepper La. C'fon 4C 4
(off Cei Banc)
Peris Av. Tow 3F 27
Peters Clo. Pres 5C 30
Peulwys Av. Old C 5E 22
Peulwys La. Old C 6D 22
Peulwys Rd. Old C 4E 22
Pine Ct. Col B 5H 21
Pine Gro. R Sea 6H 17
Pine Gro. Ct. R Sea 6H 17
Pinetree Wlk. Rhyl 5E 28
Pinfold Workshops. Rhyl 1C 32
Plas Adda. Ban 4C 10
Plas Av. Pres 3D 30
Plas Bach. Kin B 2J 27
Plas Brynmor. P'awr 2J 13
Plas Coch Ter. Beau 1J 7
(off Church St.)
Plas Cyril. Rhyl 7C 28
Plas Eithin. Col B 2H 21
Plas Foryd. Kin B 1J 27
Plas Gorphwysfa. Pres 2C 30
Plas Gwilym. Old C 4F 23
Plasllwyd Ter. Ban 2E 10
Plas Mona. L'yll 2D 8
Plas Newydd. L'no 6H 15
Plas Newydd Bldgs. Aber 5K 25
Plas Newydd Dri. Pres 3K 29
Plas Penrhyn. Pen B 5D 16
Plas Rd. L'no 2F 15
Plas Rd. Rhyl 6E 28
Plastirion. Tow 4E 26
Plastirion Av. Pres 3D 30
Plastirion Dri. Pres 3E 30
Plastirion Pk. Tow 4E 26
Plas Tre Marl. Llan J 4J 19
Plas Tudno. Pen B 5D 16
Plas Twthill. C'fon 4D 4
(off Pentre Newydd)
Plas Uchaf Av. Pres 4D 30
Plas Wylfa. Col B 4D 22
Plas-y-Brenin. Rhud 5F 33
Plas-y-Brenin. Rhud 6B 28
Plas y Bryn. Aber 7J 25
Plas y Gerddi. Ban 2G 11
Pleasant Pl. Aber 5K 25
Pleasant St. L'no 4J 15
Pleasant Vw. Old C 4F 23
Pont Rewle. C'fon 3C 4
(off Pretoria Ter.)
Pont y Ffridd. C'fon 4C 4
Pool La. Con 5F 19
Pool St. L'chan 5B 12
Poplar Gro. Pres 3B 30
Poplars Dri. Rhyl 7D 28
Porth Waterloo. C'fon 1E 4
Porth-y-Llys. Rhyl 6F 29
Powys Rd. L'no 5H 15
Prestatyn-Dyserth Walkway.
Pres 5D 30
Prestatyn Rd. Pres 2E 30
Pretoria Ter. C'fon 4C 4
Primrose Hill. St G 3A 36
Primrose Pas. L'no 4K 15
Prince Edward Av. Rhyl 6C 28
Princes Av. Pres 4C 30
Princes Dri. Col B 2J 21
Princes Dri. L'no 4K 15
Princes Pk. Rhud 6F 33
Princess Av. R Sea 7G 17
Princess Ct. Col B 2K 21
Princess Elizabeth Av. Rhyl 5D 28
Princess Rd. Old C 4D 22
Princes St. Rhyl 6C 28
Promenade. Aber 3J 25
Promenade. Col B 2A 22
Promenade. Deg 1F 19
Promenade. L'no 3E 14
Promenade. L'chan 4B 12
Promenade. Pres 3H 29
Promenade, The. Kin B 2G 27
Promenade, The. L'no 2G 15
Prospect Ter. L'no 2F 15
Purbeck Av. Pres 3A 30
Pwll-y-Bont. Pres 6B 30
Pwllycrochan Av. Col B 3J 21
Pydew Rd. Bryn P 3B 20
Pyllau Rd. L'no 1E 14

Q

Quay St. Rhyl 1K 27
Queen Elizabeth Ct. L'no 4J 15
Queen Av. Col B 3K 21
Queens Av. Old C 3E 22
Queen's Dri. Col B 3J 21
Queens Gdns. L'no 5J 15
Queens Pk. Col B 3K 21
Queens Rd. Aber 5J 25
Queen's Rd. L'no 6J 15
Queen's Rd. Llan J 5K 19
Queen's Rd. Old C 3E 22
Queens Shop. Cen. Rhyl 5B 28
Queen St. Rhyl 6B 28
Queen's Wlk. Rhyl 5C 28
Queensway. Aber 3K 25
Queensway. L'no 5J 15
Queensway. Old C 3E 22
Queensway. Pres 3D 30

R

Rachel Dri. Rhyl 1F 33
Raglan St. Beau 2K 7
Rathbone Pas. L'no 3F 15
Rathbone Ter. Deg 2G 19
Rating Row. Beau 1J 7
Rayleigh Av. Old C 4C 22
Rectory La. Gwae 6F 31
Rectory La. L'no 3F 15
Red Gables. P'awr 2H 13
Red Hill. St As 5C 38
Redlands Clo. Pen B 5B 16
Redwood Dri. Rhyl 5D 28
Rees Av. Rhyl 5D 28
Reform St. L'no 3G 15
Regent Rd. Rhyl 5D 28
Regent St. Ban 2D 10
Rhes Alexandra. C'fon 3D 4
(off Stryd William)
Rhes Clarke. C'fon 4D 4
(off Lon Ysgol Rad, in two parts)
Rhes Gwstenin. C'fon 5D 4
Rhes Penllys. Ban 2D 10
Rhes Priordy. C'fon 4C 4
(off Pretoria Ter.)
Rhes Segontiwm. C'fon 4C 4
Rhes Seiriol. Ban 1F 11
Rhes Tan-y-Bryn. Ban 3E 10
Rhes Tan-y-Bryn. L'no 4K 15
Rhiw Grange. Col B 4A 22
Rhiwlas. Aber 6J 25
Rhiwledyn. L'no 3B 16
Rhiw Rd. Col B 4K 21
Rhodfa Anwyl. Rhud 4E 32
Rhodfa Arthur. Trel 2H 35
Rhodfa Bedwen. Pres 2F 31
Rhodfa Belmont. Ban 3B 10
Rhodfa Celyn. Pres 2F 31
Rhodfa Conwy. Dys 2B 34
Rhodfa Cregyn. Ban 5B 26
Rhodfa Criccieth. Bod 3F 37
Rhodfa Derwen. Pres 2F 31
Rhodfa Ganol. Pres 7B 30
Rhodfa Glenys. St As 5C 38
Rhodfa Gofer. Dys 2B 34
Rhodfa Gop. Trel 2J 35
Rhodfa Graig. Pres 7B 30
Rhodfa Greenwood. Ban 3F 11
Rhodfa Heilyn. Dys 2B 34
Rhodfa Hendre. Pres 7B 30
Rhodfa Kingsley. Ban 3F 11
Rhodfa Lwyd. L'faen 5K 23
Rhodfa Maen Gwyn. Rhyl 7F 29
Rhodfa Maes Hir. Rhyl 7F 29
Rhodfa Menai. Ban 2C 10
Rhodfa Nant. Tow 5F 27
Rhodfa Pedr. Dys 2B 34
Rhodfa Penrhos. Ban 5A 10
Rhodfa Penrhyn. Ban 4F 11
Rhodfa Plas. Pres 7B 30
Rhodfa Plas Coed. Rhyl 6F 29
Rhodfa'r Esgob. Ban 2E 10
Rhodfa'r Frenhines. Ban 4F 11
Rhodfa'r Grug. Col B 4J 21
Rhodfa Ronald. Bod 2E 36
Rhodfa'r Paun. Ban 1E 10
Rhodfa Sant Elian. Col B 6D 22
Rhodfa Sian. Dys 4B 34
Rhodfa Sychnant. Con 6E 18
Rhodfa Wen. L'faen 6K 23
Rhodfa Wyn. Pres 2A 30

Rhos Fawr. *Aber* 5B **26**
Rhosfryn. *Ban* 7J **9**
Rhos Gwyn. *Old C* 4E **22**
Rhos Ind. Pk. *R Sea* 6G **17**
Rhoslan. *Rho* 4G **5**
Rhoslan Pk. *Col B* 2K **21**
Rhos Manor. *R Sea* 6J **17**
Rhos Promenade. *R Sea* 7J **17**
Rhos Rd. *R Sea* 7G **17**
Rhos Uchaf. *Ban* 6K **9**
Rhos-y-Gad. *L'yll* 3D **8**
Rhuddlan Av. *L'no* 5H **15**
Rhuddlan Rd. *Aber* 6K **25**
Rhuddlan Rd. *Bod* 3F **37**
Rhuddlan Rd. *Rhyl* 7D **28**
Rhyd Dri. *R Sea* 5G **17**
Rhyd Menai. *Men B* 2J **9**
Rhydwen Clo. *Rhyl* 1B **32**
Rhydwen Dri. *Rhyl* 7A **28**
Rhyd-y-Foel Rd. *L'las* 7C **24**
Rhyl Coast Rd. *Rhyl* 4D **28**
Rhyl Rd. *Rhud* 5E **32**
Rhys Av. *Kin B* 2G **27**
Rhys Evans Clo. *Pen B* 5D **16**
Ridgway Av. *Rhyl* 4E **28**
Riverside Clo. *Kin B* 2J **27**
Riverside Ct. *Deg* 1F **19**
River St. *Rhyl* 6A **28**
River Vw. Ter. Llan J 5K **19**
(off Ffordd Maelgwn)
Riviere Av. *L'no* 4J **15**
Riviere's Av. *Col B* 3K **21**
Rochester Dri. *Pres* 4B **30**
Rochester Way. *R Sea* 6G **17**
Rockfield Dri. *L'no* 1F **19**
Rock Villa Rd. *P'awr* 2H **13**
Roe Parc. *St As* 5B **38**
Roe, The. *St As* 4B **38**
Rofft Pl. *L'no* 2F **15**
Roland Av. *Kin B* 2H **27**
Ronald Av. *Llan J* 5K **19**
Ronaldsway. *Rhyl* 1D **32**
Rosebery Av. *L'no* 4K **15**
Rosedale Gdns. *Rhyl* 1F **33**
Rose Hill. Beau 1J **7**
(off Gaol St.)
Rose Hill. *Old C* 4D **22**
Rosehill Rd. *Rhyl* 1E **32**
Rose Hill St. *Con* 6G **19**
Rosemary Av. *Col B* 4A **22**
Rosemary La. *Beau* 1J **7**
Rosemary La. *Con* 6F **19**
Rosemount Av. *Kin B* 1H **27**
Roseview Cres. *Kin B* 2J **27**
Roslin Gdns. *L'no* 4K **15**
Roumania Cres. *L'no* 4K **15**
Roumania Dri. *L'no* 4K **15**
Roundwood Av. *Pres* 6B **30**
Rowan Dri. *Rhyl* 1F **33**
Royal Welch Av. *Bod* 4E **36**
Roy Av. *Pres* 3H **29**
Royd Ter. *R Sea* 1H **21**
Ruby Ter. *St As* 6B **38**
Russell Av. *Col B* 4K **21**
Russell Dri. *Pres* 3K **29**
Russell Gdns. *Rhyl* 5C **28**
Russell Rd. *Rhyl* 6B **28**

S

St Agnes Rd. *Con* 6F **19**
St Andrew's Av. *L'no* 4F **15**
St Andrews Dri. *Pres* 4C **30**
St Andrew's Pl. *L'no* 3F **15**
St Andrews Rd. *Col B* 5J **21**
St Anne's Av. *Pres* 5A **30**
St Annes Ct. *L'no* 1J **19**
St Anne's Gdns. *L'no* 1J **19**
St Anns St. *Rhyl* 6C **28**
St Asaph Av. *Kin B* 1H **27**
St Asaph Bus. Pk. *St As* 5J **37**
St Asaph Dri. *Pres* 5B **30**
St Asaph Rd. *Dys* 5B **34**
St Asaph Rd. *Rhud* 7E **32**
St Asaph Rd. *St G* 2A **36**
(in two parts)
St Asaph St. *Rhyl* 5C **28**
St Barbara's Av. *Bod* 3D **36**
St Brelade's Dri. *Pres* 4C **30**
St Bueno's. *L'no* 2E **14**
St Catherine's Dri. *Old C* 4D **22**
St Chads Way. *Pres* 5B **30**
St David's Av. *L'no* 4K **19**
St Davids Clo. *Pen B* 5D **16**
St David's Pl. *L'no* 4G **15**
St Davids Rd. *Aber* 5H **25**

St David's Rd. *L'no* 3F **15**
St David's Rd. *Old C* 4F **23**
St Davids Rd. *P'awr* 2H **13**
St David's Rd. *Pen B* 5D **16**
St David's Sq. *Rhyl* 7C **28**
St Davids Ter. *P'awr* 2J **13**
St Elmo's Dri. *Pres* 4D **30**
St George Rd. *Aber* 6K **25**
St George's Cres. L'no 3G **15**
(off Parade, The)
St Georges Cres. *Rhyl* 5D **28**
St George's Dri. *Deg* 4H **19**
St Georges Dri. *Pres* 4C **30**
St George's Pl. *L'no* 3G **15**
St Georges Rd. *R Sea* 7H **17**
St Hilary's Ct. *Deg* 4H **19**
St Hilary's Dri. *Deg* 4H **19**
St Hilary's Rd. *L'no* 6J **15**
St James Dri. *Ban* 3D **10**
St James Dri. *Pres* 2H **13**
St Johns Cres. *Old C* 4D **22**
St Johns Pk. *P'awr* 2H **13**
St Johns Pk. E. *P'awr* 2H **13**
St Johns Pk. W. *P'awr* 2H **13**
St Margarets Av. *Pres* 5A **30**
St Margaret's Dri. *L'no* 4H **15**
St Margaret's Dri. *Rhyl* 7D **28**
St Margarets Rd. *Llan J* 5K **19**
St Mary Av. *Ban* 2E **10**
St Mary's Ct. *Rhyl* 5C **28**
St Mary's Dri. *Rhyl* 7D **28**
St Mary's Rd. *L'no* 3G **15**
St Pauls Clo. *Col B* 3K **21**
St Pauls Ter. *Ban* 3D **10**
St Seiriol's Gdns. *L'no* 4F **15**
St Seiriol's Rd. *L'no* 4F **15**
St Tudno's Rd. *L'no* 1D **14**
St Winifreds Clo. *L'chan* 5B **12**
Salem Ter. *Rhyd* 7C **24**
Salisbury Ct. *L'no* 3F **15**
Salisbury Dri. *Pres* 4A **30**
Salisbury Pas. *L'no* 3F **15**
Salisbury Rd. *L'no* 3F **15**
Sandbank Rd. *Tow* 4K **15**
Sandfield Pl. *Rhyl* 7A **28**
Sandhills Rd. *Old C* 4D **22**
Sandhurst Rd. *Pres* 3A **30**
Sandiway. *Pres* 3J **29**
Sandringham Av. *Rhyl* 6A **28**
Sandy La. *Pres* 2C **30**
San Remo Av. *Tow* 3E **26**
Sarn La. *Rhud* 2G **37**
Saunders Way. *Rhyl* 1D **32**
School La. *L'no* 3F **15**
School La. *P'awr* 2J **13**
Seabank Dri. *Pres* 3A **30**
Sea Bank Rd. *Col B* 1K **21**
Seabank Rd. *Rhyl* 7A **28**
Seafield Dri. *Aber* 6K **25**
Seafield Rd. *Col B* 4K **21**
Sea Rd. *Aber* 6K **25**
(in three parts)
Sea Rd. *Pres* 2B **30**
Sea Vw. Ct. *Kin B* 2G **27**
Sea Vw. Rd. *Col B* 2A **22**
Seaview Ter. *Con* 5G **19**
Second Av. *Pres* 1B **30**
Second Av. *R Sea* 6G **17**
Sefton Rd. *Old C* 4E **22**
Sefton Ter. *Deg* 2F **19**
Seven Sisters Rd. *Pres* 2C **30**
Seventh Av. *Col B* 5J **21**
Seymour Dri. *Rhud* 5F **33**
Shaftesbury Av. *Pen B* 5D **16**
Shamrock Ct. *Con* 3J **19**
Shamrock Ter. *Deg* 3J **19**
Shaun Clo. *Rhyl* 1E **32**
Shaun Dri. *Rhyl* 1E **32**
Sherwood Av. *Rhyl* 4H **29**
Sholing Dri. *Rhyl* 5E **28**
Shore Rd. *Gron* 1H **31**
Shore Rd. *L'chan* 4B **12**
Shore Rd. E. *L'chan* 4B **12**
Silverdale Ter. St As 5C **38**
(off Mill St.)
Singleton Cres. *Moch* 3F **21**
Sisson St. *Rhyl* 7C **28**
Skerryvore Rd. *Bryn P* 2A **20**
Smith Av. *Old C* 4C **22**
Snowden Vs. *Ban* 2D **10**
Snowdon Vw. *Ban* 2D **10**
Somerset St. *L'no* 3G **15**
South Av. *Pres* 3C **30**
South Av. *Rhyl* 7A **28**
South Dri. *Rhyl* 1E **32**
S. Kinmel St. *Rhyl* 6B **28**
Southlands Rd. *Kin B* 1J **27**

South Pde. *L'no* 2G **15**
South Pde. *Pens* 3K **25**
South Pl. *R Sea* 6H **17**
South St. *L'chan* 3C **12**
Springdale. *Col B* 6E **22**
Spring Gdns. *Aber* 5J **25**
Spruce Av. *Rhyl* 5E **28**
Square, The. *Kin B* 2H **27**
(Foryd Rd.)
Square, The. *Kin B* 3J **27**
(Park Av.)
Stad Foel Graig. *L'yll* 3E **8**
Stad Garnedd. *Star* 2A **8**
Stamford St. *Deg* 3H **19**
Stanley Oak Rd. *Llan J* 5K **19**
Stanley Pk. *Rhyl* 7E **28**
Stanley Pk. Av. *Rhyl* 7E **28**
Stanley St. *Beau* 1J **7**
Stanmore St. *Rhyl* 7A **28**
Station Rd. *Col B* 4D **22**
(Abergele Rd.)
Station Rd. *Col B* 3K **21**
(Woodland Rd. W.)
Station Rd. Deg & *Moch* 3E **20**
Station Rd. *Deg* 2F **19**
Station Rd. *L'las* 4B **24**
Station Rd. *L'chan* 4B **12**
Station Rd. *L'yll* 3D **8**
Station Rd. *Pres* 2C **30**
Station Rd. *Rhud* 6E **32**
Station Rd. E. *P'awr* 1J **13**
Station Rd. W. *P'awr* 2J **13**
Station St. *Aber* 3K **25**
Station Ter. *Llan J* 5K **19**
Steeple La. *Beau* 1J **7**
Stephen Rd. *Pres* 4J **29**
Stephenson Clo. *Con* 3E **18**
Stephenson Clo. *Pen B* 5C **16**
Stephen St. *L'no* 3G **15**
Stoneby Dri. *Rhyl* 4D **30**
Strand St. *Ban* 1F **11**
Stryd Albert. *Ban* 2D **10**
Stryd Ambrose. *Ban* 2F **11**
Stryd Bangor. *C'fon* 4C **4**
Stryd Belmont. *Ban* 3C **10**
Stryd Capel Joppa. *C'fon* 5D **4**
Stryd Clarence. *Ban* 3C **10**
Stryd Deinoi. *Ban* 2D **10**
Stryd Dinorwic. *C'fon* 4D **4**
Stryd Edmund. *Ban* 1F **11**
Stryd Fawr. *Ban* 3D **10**
Stryd Fawr. *C'fon* 4C **4**
Stryd Fawr. *Men B* 2K **9**
Stryd Fawr. *P'awr* 2G **13**
Stryd Garnon. *C'fon* 4D **4**
Stryd John Llwdd. *C'fon* 5D **4**
Stryd Marcws. *C'fon* 5D **4**
Stryd Marged. *C'fon* 4D **4**
Stryd Mari. *C'fon* 4D **4**
Stryd Mason. *C'fon* 1F **11**
Stryd Newydd. *C'fon* 4D **4**
Stryd Niwbwrch. *C'fon* 4D **4**
Stryd Pedwara Chwech. *C'fon* 4C **4**
Stryd Robert. *Ban* 1F **11**
Stryd Rolant. *C'fon* 3D **4**
Stryd Santes Helen. *C'fon* 5D **4**
Stryd Thomas. *C'fon* 4D **4**
Stryd Victoria. *Ban* 2D **10**
Stryd Victoria. *C'fon* 4D **4**
Stryd William. *Ban* 2F **11**
Stryd William. *C'fon* 4D **4**
Stryd-y-Bont. *Men B* 3K **9**
Stryd-y-Capel. *Men B* 3K **9**
Stryd y Castell. *C'fon* 4C **4**
Stryd-y-Dderwen. *Aber* 5B **26**
Stryd y Degwen. *C'fon* 4D **4**
Stryd y Deon. *Ban* 2E **10**
Stryd y Faenol. *C'fon* 4C **4**
Stryd y Farchnad. *C'fon* 4C **4**
Stryd y Ffynon. *Men B* 2K **9**
Stryd-y-Gwynt. *Con* 5F **19**
Stryd y Jel. *C'fon* 4C **4**
Stryd y Llyn. *C'fon* 4D **4**
Stryd y Pistyll. *Ban* 1F **11**
Stryd y Plas. *C'fon* 4C **4**
Stryd y Porth Mawr. *C'fon* 4C **4**
Stryd yr Allt. *Ban* 2C **10**
Stryd yr Eglwys. *C'fon* 4C **4**
Stryd yr Hendre. *C'fon* 5D **4**
Stuart Dri. *R Sea* 7G **17**
Sudbury Clo. *Rhyl* 7B **28**
Sunningdale. *Aber* 4H **25**
Sunningdale Av. *Col B* 4H **21**
Sunningdale Dri. *Pen B* 5D **16**
Sunningdale Gro. *Col B* 4J **21**
Sunray Av. *Aber* 5B **26**
Susan Gro. *Pres* 3B **30**

Sussex St. *Rhyl* 6B **28**
Swan Rd. *Moch* 4E **20**
Swn y Dail. *Bod* 3E **36**
Swn y-Don. *Col B* 5G **23**
Sycamore Cres. *Pres* 3D **30**
Sycamore Gro. *Rhyl* 5D **28**
Sychnant Pass Rd. *P'awr* 7K **13**
Sydenham Av. *Aber* 5K **25**
Sydenham Av. *Rhyl* 1K **27**
Sylva Gdns. N. *L'no* 4K **15**
Sylva Gdns. S. *L'no* 4K **15**
Sylva Gro. *L'no* 4K **15**

T

Tabor Hill. *L'no* 2F **15**
Tai Glangwna. *Cae* 6H **5**
Tai Lon. *L'yll* 3F **9**
Tair Felin. *St As* 5C **38**
Tai'r Mynydd. *Ban* 2E **10**
Talargoch Ind. Est. *Dys* 1B **34**
Taliesin St. *L'no* 3F **15**
Talton Ct. *Pres* 4E **30**
Talton Cres. *Pres* 3E **30**
Tal-y-Sarn. *Tre I* 5K **19**
Tan Benarth. *Con* 7F **19**
Tanrallt. *C'fon* 4D **4**
Tanrallt Av. *Kin B* 5K **27**
(in two parts)
Tanrallt Cotts. *D'chi* 7H **13**
Tanrallt St. *Moch* 4F **21**
Tan Refail. *Deg* 2J **19**
Tan Rhiw. *Pen B* 4D **16**
Tan-y-Berllan. *Deg* 3J **19**
Tan y Bonc. *Men B* 3K **9**
Tan y Bryn. *Ban* 5H **11**
Tan-y-Bryn. *Llan J* 4J **19**
Tan y Bryn. *R Sea* 5A **38**
Tan-y-Bryn Dri. *R Sea* 7G **17**
Tan y Bryn Rd. *L'no* 5K **15**
Tan y Bryn Rd. *R Sea* 7G **17**
Tan y Coed. *Maes* 4F **11**
Tan y Coed. *P'side* 5C **16**
Tan y Cwm. *L'no* 5G **15**
(off Maes-y-Cwm)
Tan-y-Felin. *Con* 6G **19**
Tan y Ffordd. *L'wrn* 1A **6**
Tan-y-Foel. *Rhyd* 7C **24**
Tan-y-Fron. *Col B* 5B **22**
Tan-y-Fron. *Deg* 3H **19**
Tan-y-Fyn Went. *Ban* 2E **10**
Tan-y-Gaer. *Aber* 6H **25**
Tan-y-Gaer. *Deg* 2J **19**
Tan-y-Gopa Rd. *Aber* 6H **25**
Tan y Graig. *Ban* 4C **10**
Tan y Graig. *L'yll* 3D **8**
Tan-y-Lan Rd. *Old C* 3F **23**
Tan y Maes. *Ban* 4D **10**
Tan y Maes. *Llan J* 4A **20**
Tan y-Maes. *Pres* 7C **30**
Tan y Marian. *L'las* 5B **24**
Tan-y-Marian Clo. *Gron* 3K **31**
Tan y Mur. C'fon 4C **4**
(off Stryd yr Eglwys)
Tan-y-Mynydd. *Ban* 3F **11**
Tan-yr-Allt Av. *Moch* 3F **21**
Tan-yr-Allt Rd. *L'las* 4A **24**
Tan-yr-Eglwys Rd. *Rhud* 5E **32**
Tan-yr-Ogof Rd. *L'no* 2F **15**
Tan-y-Wylfa. *Aber* 6H **25**
Tan-y-Wal. *Old C* 3F **23**
Tarleton St. *Rhyl* 5C **28**
Tarquin Dri. *Rhyl* 1F **33**
Taverners Ct. *L'no* 4F **15**
Tegfan. *Aber* 5B **26**
Telford Clo. *Con* 3E **18**
Tennis Ct. Rd. *Aber* 5A **26**
Terfyn Pella Av. *Rhyl* 3H **29**
Terrace Wlk. *L'chan* 7B **12**
(in two parts)
Terrence Av. *Rhyl* 7B **28**
Third Av. *Pres* 1B **30**
Thomas Av. *Dys* 3B **34**
Thomas Clo. *Beau* 1H **7**
Thornley Av. *Rhyl* 3H **15**
Thornley Av. *Rhyl* 7E **28**
Thornton Clo. *Rhyl* 7B **28**
Thorpe St. *L'no* 4G **15**
Thorpe St. *Rhyl* 6C **28**
Tip La. *Pres* 4B **30**
Tir Estyn. *Deg* 3J **19**
Tir Llwyd Enterprise Pk.
Tir Llwyd Ind. Est. *Kin B* 6J **27**

Tom White Ct. *Pen B* . . . 5C 16
Toronnen. *Ban* . . . 6B 10
Tower Ct. *Rhyl* . . . 1D 32
Tower Gdns. *Rhyl* . . . 1D 32
Tower Way. *Aber* . . . 6K 25
Town Ditch Rd. *Con* . . . 5F 19
Townsend. *Beau* . . . 2J 7
Towyn Rd. *Aber* . . . 5A 26
Towyn Way E. *Tow* . . . 4G 27
Towyn Way W. *Tow* . . . 5E 26
Traeth Melyn. *Deg* . . . 1F 19
Traeth Penrhyn. *Pen B* . . . 3E 16
Trafford Pk. *Pen B* . . . 5D 16
Trawscoed Rd. *L'faen* . . . 7K 23
Tre Borth. *Pres* . . . 2C 30
Tree Tops Ct. *Rhud* . . . 5F 33
Treflan. *Ban* . . . 3D 10
Trefnant Av. *Kin B* . . . 3J 27
Trefonwys. *Ban* . . . 3B 10
Trefor Av. *Ban* . . . 2G 27
Treforris Rd. *D'chi* . . . 7H 13
Tregaean. *P'edd* . . . 5K 9
Trehearn Dri. *Rhyl* . . . 5D 28
Trehwfa. *Ban* . . . 5B 10
Trellewelyn Clo. *Rhyl* . . . 7E 28
Trellewelyn Rd. Rhyl . . . 7F 29
(Colin Dri.)
Trellewelyn Rd. Rhyl . . . 7D 28
(Rhuddlan Rd.)
Trem Arfon. *L'fan* . . . 5B 6
Tre Marl Ind. Est. *Tre I* . . . 5A 20
Trem Cinmel. *Tow* . . . 4F 27
Trem Elidir. *Ban* . . . 4B 10
Trem Elwy. *Kin B* . . . 2H 27
Trem Eryri. *L'yll* . . . 3D 8
Trem Eryri. *Men B* . . . 2J 9
Trem-y-Bont. *Kin B* . . . 2J 27
Trem-y-Castell. *Tow* . . . 5E 26
Trem-y-Don. *L'faen* . . . 5K 23
Trem-y-Dyffryn. *Kin B* . . . 4K 27
Trem-y-Ffair. *Kin B* . . . 2H 27
Trem-y-Foryd. *Kin B* . . . 2J 27
Trem-y-Garnedd. *Ban* . . . 4F 11
Trem-y-Geulan. *Kin B* . . . 2J 27
Trem-y-Mor. *Aber* . . . 6H 25
Trem-y-Mynydd. *Aber* . . . 5B 26
Trem-yr-Afon. *Kin B* . . . 2J 27
Trem yr Afon. *Llan J* . . . 5A 20
Trem-yr-Harbwr. *Kin B* . . . 2J 27
Tre r Felin. *Ban* . . . 5J 11
Tre r Gof. *C'fon* . . . 4D 4
Trevor Av. *Rhud* . . . 4F 33
Trevor Av. *Rhyl* . . . 1D 32
Trevor Rd. *Col B* . . . 3B 22
Trevor Rd. *Pres* . . . 2C 30
Trevor St. *L'no* . . . 3G 15
Trillo Av. *R Sea* . . . 6J 17
Trinity Av. *L'no* . . . 4F 15
Trinity Ct. *L'no* . . . 4F 15
Trinity Ct. *Rhyl* . . . 6B 28
(off Russell Rd.)
Trinity Cres. *L'no* . . . 5E 14
Trinity Sq. *L'no* . . . 3G 15
Troed-y-Bwlch. *Deg* . . . 2H 19
Troon Clo. *Col B* . . . 4J 21
Troon Way. *Aber* . . . 5H 25
Troon Way. *Col B* . . . 4J 21
Tudno Av. *Pres* . . . 3E 30
Tudor Av. *Rhyl* . . . 7D 28
Tudor Ct. *L'no* . . . 3H 15
(off Tudor Rd.)
Tudor Gro. *Kin B* . . . 3H 27
Tudor Pk. *Kin B* . . . 5J 27
Tudor Rd. *L'no* . . . 3H 15
Turf Sq. *C'fon* . . . 4C 4
Turnberry Dri. *Aber* . . . 5H 25
Twll yn y Wal. *C'fon* . . . 4C 4
Ty-Coch Rd. *L'no* . . . 2F 15
Tyddyn Ddeici. *L'yll* . . . 3E 8
Tyddyn Drycin. *L'chan* . . . 3C 12
Tyddyn Isaf. *Men B* . . . 1J 9
Tyddyn Llwydyn. *C'fon* . . . 6E 4

Tyddyn Mostyn. *Men B* . . . 2J 9
Tyddyn Nicholas. *Men B* . . . 2J 9
Tyddyn To. *Men B* . . . 2J 9
Ty Gwyn Gdns. *Con* . . . 6F 19
Ty Gwyn Jones. *Aber* . . . 6K 25
Ty-Gwyn Rd. *L'no* . . . 1E 14
Ty-Isa Rd. *L'no* . . . 2G 15
Ty Mawr. *Men B* . . . 2J 9
Ty Mawr. Rd. *Con* . . . 3G 19
Tyn Cae. *L'yll* . . . 3D 8
Ty'n Caeau. *L'yll* . . . 3D 8
Tynewydd Rd. *Rhyl* . . . 4E 28
Ty'n-y-Cae. *L'yll* . . . 3D 8
Ty'n-y-Coed Rd. *L'no* . . . 2E 14
Tyn y Ffrith Rd. *L'no* . . . 3J 15
Ty'n-y-Fron Rd. *Llan J* . . . 5K 19
Tyn-y-Maes. *L'faen* . . . 5K 23
Tyn-y-Maes Hill. *L'no* . . . 2F 15
Tywyn Ganol. *Pres* . . . 3B 30

U

Upland Rd. *Col B* . . . 4A 22
Up. Bryn Owen Ter. *Ban* . . . 5C 10
Up. Bryntirion Dri. *Pres* . . . 4D 30
Up. Denbigh Rd. *St As* . . . 6C 38
Up. Dys Rd. *Dys* . . . 5B 34
Up. Foel Rd. *Dys* . . . 5B 34
Up. Gate St. *Con* . . . 6F 19
Up. Maenan. *P'awr* . . . 2H 13
Up. Mill Rd. *L'chan* . . . 6C 12
Up. Promenade. *Col B* . . . 1J 21
Up. Water St. *P'awr* . . . 2G 13
Uwych-y-Don Av. *Col B* . . . 4F 23
Uxbridge Sq. *C'fon* . . . 4D 4

V

Vale Pk. *Rhyl* . . . 7C 28
Vale Rd. *Llan J* . . . 5J 19
Vale Rd. *Rhyl* . . . 6C 28
Vale Rd. Bri. *Rhyl* . . . 6B 28
Vale Rd. Vw. Ter. *Rhyl* . . . 6C 28
Valley Rd. *L'chan* . . . 5C 12
Vardre Av. *Deg* . . . 3G 19
Vardre Clo. *Deg* . . . 2H 19
Vardre La. *L'no* . . . 2G 15
Vardre Pk. *Deg* . . . 2H 19
Vardre Vw. Ter. *Deg* . . . 3H 19
Vaughan Clo. *Pres* . . . 4C 30
Vaughan St. *L'no* . . . 4G 15
Vaughan St. *Rhyl* . . . 6B 28
Vezey St. *Rhyl* . . . 6C 28
Vicarage Av. *L'no* . . . 6J 15
Vicarage Clo. *Bod* . . . 3F 37
Vicarage Clo. *L'no* . . . 6J 15
Vicarage Gdns. *L'no* . . . 6J 15
Vicarage La. *Rhud* . . . 4E 32
Vicarage Rd. *L'no* . . . 6J 15
Victoria Av. *Ban* . . . 2D 10
Victoria Av. *Col B* . . . 2A 22
Victoria Av. *L'no* . . . 3K 15
Victoria Av. *Pres* . . . 3D 30
Victoria Av. *Rhyl* . . . 7A 28
Victoria Cen. *L'no* . . . 3G 15
Victoria Cres. *Llan J* . . . 4J 19
Victoria Dri. *Llan J* . . . 5J 19
Victoria Gdns. *Col B* . . . 4K 21
Victoria La. *Pres* . . . 3B 30
Victoria Pk. *Col B* . . . 2H 21
Victoria Pk. Av. *Pres* . . . 2B 30
Victoria Pk. Rd. *Old C* . . . 4D 22
Victoria Pk. *Pres* . . . 3K 29
Victoria Rd. *Rhyl* . . . 7C 28
Victoria Rd. W. *Pres* . . . 4H 29
Victoria Sq. *Ban* . . . 4C 10
Victoria St. *L'no* . . . 3J 15
Victoria Ter. *Beau* . . . 1K 7
Victoria Ter. *P'awr* . . . 2G 13
Victor Rd. *Col B* . . . 3A 22
Victor Wilde Dri. *R Sea* . . . 6H 17
Village Rd. *L'chan* . . . 5B 12
Village, The. *Bod* . . . 3F 37

Vincent Av. *L'no* . . . 5J 15
Vincent Clo. *Rhyl* . . . 5D 28
Vinton Pl. *Col B* . . . 6E 22
Viola Av. *Rhyl* . . . 1D 32
Violet Gro. *Rhyl* . . . 7F 29
Voel Rd. *P'awr* . . . 2K 13
Voryn Av. *Old C* . . . 3F 23

W

Waen Rd. *Glan* . . . 1C 20
Waen Ter. *Con* . . . 4E 18
Walford Av. *Rhyl* . . . 7C 28
Walshaw Av. *Col B* . . . 2J 21
Walton Cres. *Llan J* . . . 5K 19
Walton Rd. *Llan J* . . . 4K 19
Ward Clo. *Pen B* . . . 5C 16
Warehouse St. *L'no* . . . 4G 15
War Memorial Ct. *Rhyl* . . . 6D 28
Warren Clo. *Pres* . . . 1E 30
Warren Dri. *Deg* . . . 3H 19
Warren Dri. *Pres* . . . 2E 30
Warren Rd. *Deg* . . . 3H 19
Warren Rd. *Pres* . . . 2D 30
Warren Rd. *Pres* . . . 7A 28
Washington Ct. *Rhyl* . . . 1E 32
Waterfall Rd. *Dys* . . . 2B 34
Waterloo St. *Ban* . . . 2E 10
Water St. *Aber* . . . 5K 25
Water St. *L'no* . . . 2F 15
Water St. *P'awr* . . . 2G 13
Water St. *Rhyl* . . . 6B 28
Watkin Av. *Old C* . . . 4E 22
Watkin St. *Con* . . . 5F 19
Weaver Av. *Rhyl* . . . 7E 28
Weavers La. *Dys* . . . 3B 34
Weaverton Dri. *Rhyl* . . . 1E 32
Wellfield Shop. Cen. *Ban* . . . 2E 10
Wellington Rd. *Old C* . . . 4D 22
Wellington Rd. *Rhyl* . . . 1K 27
Wellington Ter. *C'fon* . . . 5D 4
Wellington Ter. *Rhyl* . . . 7A 28
Well La. *Gwae* . . . 6E 30
(in two parts)
Wells Clo. *Pres* . . . 4A 30
Well St. *Trel* . . . 2J 35
Wendover Av. *Tow* . . . 4E 26
Wenfro. *Aber* . . . 6K 25
Wentworth Av. *Aber* . . . 5J 25
Wentworth Av. *Col B* . . . 4J 21
Wern Cres. *Moch* . . . 3F 21
Wernlas. *Aber* . . . 5B 26
Wern Rd. *L'las* . . . 4A 24
Wern y Wylan. *L'no* . . . 4G 15
West Av. *Pres* . . . 3E 30
Westbourne Av. *Rhyl* . . . 7A 28
West Clo. *Pres* . . . 3H 29
Westdale Ct. *Rhud* . . . 5E 32
West End. *Ban* . . . 4C 10
West End. *Beau* . . . 2J 7
W. End Hill. *L'no* . . . 3F 15
Westfield Rd. *Rhyl* . . . 6C 28
W. Kinmel St. *Rhyl* . . . 7B 28
Westminster Av. *Rhyl* . . . 7E 28
Weston Ct. *Rhyl* . . . 4E 28
Weston Rd. *Rhyl* . . . 7B 28
West Pde. *L'no* . . . 3E 14
West Pde. *Rhyl* . . . 1K 27
West Promenade. *R Sea* . . . 7J 17
West Rd. *Old C* . . . 4E 22
W. Shore. *L'chan* . . . 4A 12
West St. *Rhyl* . . . 7A 28
Westwood Cvn. Pk. *L'faen* . . . 5J 23
Wexham St. *Beau* . . . 1J 7
Whinacres. *Con* . . . 4E 18
Whiston Pas. *L'no* . . . 3F 15
Whitehall Rd. *R Sea* . . . 1H 21
Whiterose Clo. *Pres* . . . 2C 30
Williams St. *Rhyl* . . . 7C 28
William's Ter. *L'yll* . . . 3D 8
Willoughby Rd. *R Sea* . . . 1H 21
Willowbrook. *Col B* . . . 7E 22
Willow Clo. *Col B* . . . 6E 22

Willow Ct. *Rhyl* . . . 1J 27
Willow Ct. *Rhyl* . . . 5E 28
Willows, The. *Pres* . . . 3K 29
Winchester Clo. *R Sea* . . . 6F 17
Winchester Dri. *Pres* . . . 4A 30
Windermere Dri. *Pres* . . . 2B 30
Windsor Dri. *Old C* . . . 4C 22
Windsor Gro. *Kin B* . . . 3H 27
Windsor Pas. *L'no* . . . 3G 15
Windsor St. *Rhyl* . . . 6B 28
Winllan Av. *L'no* . . . 4F 15
Winnard Av. *Rhyl* . . . 7A 28
Winston Clo. *Old C* . . . 4F 23
Withington Av. *Old C* . . . 4D 22
Woodbine Ter. *P'side* . . . 5C 16
Woodend Dri. *Old C* . . . 4E 22
Woodfield Av. *Col B* . . . 4A 22
Woodhill Rd. *Col B* . . . 3K 21
Woodland Av. *Old C* . . . 4E 22
Woodland Pk. *Col B* . . . 3K 21
Woodland Pk. W. *Col B* . . . 3K 21
Woodland Rd. E. *Col B* . . . 3K 21
Woodland Rd. W. *Col B* . . . 3K 21
Woodlands. *Llan J* . . . 3J 19
Woodlands Av. *R Sea* . . . 7J 17
Wood Rd. *Rhyl* . . . 7A 28
Woodside Av. *Kin B* . . . 2G 27
Woodside Gdns. *Rhyl* . . . 1D 32
Worcester Dri. *Pres* . . . 4B 30
Wormhout Way. *L'no* . . . 6J 15
Wyddfyd Rd. *L'no* . . . 2F 15
Wynn Av. *Old C* . . . 4E 22
Wynn Av. N. *Old C* . . . 4E 30
Wynn Cres. *Old C* . . . 4E 22
Wynn Dri. *Old C* . . . 4E 22
Wynne Clo. *Rhud* . . . 6F 33
Wynn Gdns. *Old C* . . . 4E 22
Wynnstay Av. *Pres* . . . 2K 21
Wynnstay Rd. *Col B* . . . 4E 22

Y

Y Berllan. *P'awr* . . . 2J 13
Y Bryn. *Gla C* . . . 7B 20
Y Cilgant. *Ban* . . . 2D 10
Y Clogwyn. *C'fon* . . . 3D 4
Y Ddol. *Aber* . . . 5B 26
Yerburgh Av. *Col B* . . . 2H 21
Y-Felin. *Con* . . . 6G 19
Y Ffrith. *Rhyl* . . . 5D 28
Y Garnedd. *L'yll* . . . 2D 8
Y Gelli. *L'las* . . . 4B 24
Y Glyn. *C'fon* . . . 3E 4
Y Glyn. *Llan J* . . . 4J 19
Y Glyn. *Men B* . . . 2J 9
Y Gorlan. *Maes* . . . 4F 11
Y Gorlan. *Rhyl* . . . 5C 28
Y Maes. *Ban* . . . 2E 10
Y Maes. *C'fon* . . . 4C 4
York Clo. *Pres* . . . 4A 30
York Pl. *Ban* . . . 2E 10
York Pl. *Con* . . . 5G 19
York Rd. *Col B* . . . 3K 21
York Rd. *Deg* . . . 2F 19
York Rd. *L'no* . . . 3F 15
Yr Angorfa. *Con* . . . 3E 18
Yr Encil. *Aber* . . . 6A 26
Y Rhos. *Ban* . . . 6K 9
Yr Hwylfa. *C'fon* . . . 3E 4
Ysgoldy Ter. *Cap G* . . . 7H 9
Ysguborwen Rd. *D'chi* . . . 6G 13
Y Sgwar. *Men B* . . . 2K 9
Ystad Ddiwydiannol Cibyn.
   C'fon . . . 4G 5
Ystad Glandwr. *Cae* . . . 6G 5
Y Wenallt. *Aber* . . . 7J 25
Y Wern. *L'yll* . . . 2E 8

Z

Zion Pas. *L'no* . . . 3G 15